Ukrainian Easter Recipes

TRADITIONAL VELYKDEN

Third Edition

Svitlana Yakovenko

ISBN: 978-0-6489485-1-3 (Paperback, third edition)

ISBN: 978-0-9945334-3-2 (EPUB, first edition)

Cover illustration: Roksolana Panchyshyn
Design assistance: Yanitsa Slavcheva
Drawings: Ovidiu Ambrozie Bortã
Editorial assistance: Julian Grodzicky
Text, photography and ornaments: Svitlana Yakovenko

Third Edition

Illustrated

Acknowledgement

Our sincere thanks go to the wonderful staff of the National Art Museum of Ukraine, especially Lesia Tolstova and Yuliya Lytvynets, who advised on, selected and supplied copies of the Ukrainian artworks that are included in this edition. The original artworks are located in the National Art Museum of Ukraine, Kyiv.

Recipes

Paska, Baba or Babka – Velykden Bread

Borshch and Soup

Eggs and Cheese

Meats

Salads

Relishes, Sauces and Dressings

Savoury Baked Goods and Desserts

Pyrizhky Fillings

Home-Made Pantry Staples

Glossary

Bibliography

More Titles from Sova Books

Tradition on a Plate Series

Articles

Velykden – Ukrainian Easter

Springtime heralds one of the most gorgeous festive celebrations in the calendar – Easter. In Ukrainian, Easter is 'Velykden'. When literally translated 'Velykden' means 'great day'. In prehistoric times, spring's arrival was much anticipated. The ancestors of modern Ukrainians recognised a whole cycle of festive days to celebrate the spring and its sun and everything that came with it: warmer weather, the rebirth of nature, the return of favourite birds, longer days and, of course, the opportunity to access and enjoy food more easily and even stockpile it for the next cold season. Velykden is thought to be the culminating feast in those celebrations, a marker of the final victory of the Sun over the dark and cold forces of winter.

Velykden is celebrated widely throughout Ukraine and Ukrainian communities overseas. It is full of ancient pre-Christian traditions dedicated to celebrating spring's arrival, as well as a vibrant Christian tradition observing the life of Christ. It also has significance to the dedicated appreciator of rich *paska*, delicious *kovbasa*, breath-taking horseradish relish, and other scrumptious dishes.

Like many other religious holidays in Ukraine, Easter combines features of Ukraine's prevailing religion, Christianity, and the preceding system of ancient beliefs based on worshipping nature. This celebration of both the resurrection of Jesus Christ and Nature's awakening as spring arrives is what makes the Ukrainian celebration of Easter so unique, bright in its colours, meaningful in its rituals and inexhaustible in its aromas and flavours.

Unlike Rizdvo (Christmas), which is annually celebrated on 7 January, Easter does not fall on any particular date. Its timing is connected with occurrence of the Vernal (Spring) Equinox, and it is always celebrated on a Sunday.

In Ukrainian culture, Easter Sunday or Velykden is the peak of the ancient festive days. An array of customs and rituals that precede and follow the event are outlined in this book, especially where they relate to food.

Easter is preceded by Great Lent, which is the longest Lent (religious observance) in a year. During Lent, in addition to spiritual and religious pursuits, the believers adhere to a strict diet. The diet excludes sweets, meat and animal by-products, which include milk, eggs, butter and so on. Younger children, pregnant women, old and ill people were, however, permitted to have some milk or other products, if needed, to obtain some additional nutrition. The last week of Lent, known as Holy Week, is the time when, in readiness for the breaking of the strict diet, special traditional dishes are prepared for Easter celebration: *paska*, *krashanky* and *shynka or buzhenyna*.

At midnight on Easter Saturday or early Easter Sunday morning, people attend the special Resurrection Service (also, Easter Vigil). In addition to the obvious religious significance the service has a culinary connection because at this service the parishioners bring in their baskets with food to be blessed. Later, when they return home, this food is the first that they eat, thus breaking their fast. This custom is called *rozhovyny*. After *rozhovyny* the believers can eat as much buttery, meaty and fatty foods as they wish – or as their liver permits. The main foods that are included in the Easter baskets are *paska*, *krashanky*, *kovbasa*, horseradish, butter and salt (see 'Velykden Koshyk – the Easter Basket' on page 46).

The ritual of *rozhovyny* constitutes a part of the whole series of customs and traditions for the day, including special Easter greetings, an exchange of *pysanky* and *krashanky*, the sharing of *paska* and other blessed food with farm animals and, of course, the Easter meal. The traditional Easter meal is lavish and consists of foods that were not permitted during the Great Lent: eggs, meat and cheese dishes, as well as goods baked with a great deal of butter, egg yolks, milk and fragrant spices.

When the family comes home from the Resurrection Service it is still quite early in the morning. So the meal after the *rozhovyny* ritual starts as a breakfast. It then turns into brunch, lunch and dinner as families visit their relatives and neighbours and continue to be invited to join their hosts' festive meals. In some regions of Ukraine, this custom lasts for three days. Often, a family starts their visits with calling on an unwell neighbour or relative, and then they visit their other relatives and friends over the next few days. In Verkhovyna, they repeat the *rozhovyny* ritual for three days as well. In other words, each morning they start their breakfast with the food that was blessed in church.

Detail of "Easter Morning Prayer" by Mykola Pymonenko. The painting is located in the National Art Museum of Ukraine, Kyiv.

There is an old belief that is still popular among the Ukrainian villagers: no matter how much you want to sleep after *rozhovyny* (which is understandable, as the night was spent attending the church service), you must avoid having a siesta at any cost. Otherwise the summer will be dry, which will result in a poor harvest.

In case you happen to be in Ukraine during the Easter celebrations, here is one more ritual. For the whole period of Easter observances, starting with the Resurrection Service and up until the Ascension of Jesus, which takes place 40 days after the Easter Sunday, instead of the usual everyday greetings such as "Dobryi den" ('Good day') or "Pryvit" ('Hello') people great each other "Khrystos Voskres!" ('Christ is risen'), to which the whole congregation responds "Voistynu Voskres!" ('Indeed, He is risen').

Paska, Baba or Babka - Velykden Bread

Paska is a yeast-based bread that is rich with eggs and butter. It is tall and cylindrical in shape. Its rounded top is decorated with special ornaments made from dough or glazed with frosting (also, glaze or icing). The dough ornaments may include crosses, figures of birds, especially larks, and the geometrical ornaments typical of Trypillian culture, like a tryhver – a symbol with three rays originating from one dot, and curled in the same direction.

There are many recipes for *pasky*. Klynovetska's cookbook *Food and Beverages in Ukraine*, which was published in 1913, includes 16 recipes. Ten *paska* recipes are presented in this book, including some that are based on rye or cheese. Usually, when a cook finds the recipe that works for her, she adheres to it each year.

Paska, baba or babka

Paska – the Specialty Bread for Ukrainian Easter

Ukrainian cooks bake *paska* only once a year – on the occasion of Easter. *Paska* is also known as *baba* or *babka* (in this book the three words are used interchangeably). The *paska* is not just one of the attributes of the Ukrainian Easter celebrations; *paska* is a ritual in itself. The preparation, baking, blessing and eating of *paska* are accompanied by many colourful customs and beliefs.

Customarily, cooks bake several *pasky* of various sizes for each member of the family with one big *paska* to be shared by all. This *paska* is taken to church to be blessed during the Easter Vigil along with other items. The blessed *paska* is then placed in the centre of the table surrounded by *pysanky* or *krashanky* and periwinkle or myrtle, which were also blessed in the church. The blessed *paska* has many purposes. People start their Easter breakfast with it, thus breaking their fast. One custom that still survives in some regions of Ukraine is to give a piece of *paska* to all the household and farm animals in the belief that this will procure their health and wellbeing.

Making *pasky* was considered to be a great art, taking into account the old-type peel ovens, (Ukr., 'pich') that were used in the past. Even skilled cooks sometimes failed in mastering the recipe and the *paska* would not rise at all, crack or collapse. Many rituals and beliefs, now almost forgotten, are connected with the making of *pasky*. First of all, it should be quiet and peaceful in the house when *pasky* are being made. The doors should be open or closed very quietly and only if it is unavoidable. No family member should sit down in the house while the *paska* was being baked, otherwise it was believed that

the *paska* would stay 'sitting' and not rise. (In modern times the 'do not sit down' custom is still practised but the time is reduced to at least the first 15 minutes, from the time that the *paska* was placed into the oven). In short, the best conditions for baking *paska* were for the cook to be left alone in her house to go on with her task.

Depending on the traditions of the particular area, women began to bake *pasky* either on Maundy Thursday, Good Friday or Holy Saturday. Good Friday is the least popular day since many believe that it is inappropriate to bake *pasky*, as well as to perform any other household chores on the day, as it is the day when the Passion of Jesus Christ is mourned. With pure thoughts, clean clothes and prayers the cooks made their dough. Prayers or ancient spells also accompanied *pasky*, as they were placed into or removed from the oven. No one is allowed to eat *paska* before it is blessed, in other words, before Easter – even the cook herself should not taste the *paska*.

A beautifully baked golden *paska* foretells a prosperous upcoming year for the cook and her family. Accordingly, an imperfect *paska* means that the year ahead will not bring much fortune. An associated, rather gloomy, belief was that if the dough fails to rise or collapses, or the *paska* cracks when removed from the oven, it means that a family member will die during the year.

There are a few places in Ukraine, for example, in Verkhovyna, as well as some Ukrainian communities overseas, such as in Canada, where they differentiate between *paska* and *babka* and regard them as two types of Easter breads. In this instance, *paska* is a shorter round-shaped bread with dough ornaments on top, while *babka* is a tall, delicate, sweet bread with a rounded top and white icing.

Tips for Making Paska

Diversity of ingredients: Paska dough is very rich in butter and egg yolks. Its other basic ingredients include flour, yeast, sugar and milk or cream. The rest of the ingredients that are used to make *paska* are quite diverse and include: raisins, walnuts, honey, vanilla and almond extract, cinnamon, candied orange peel, lemon and orange zest, chocolate, saffron, cardamom, cloves, mace, lemon, rose extract and others.

Temperature of ingredients: All the ingredients used in *paska* dough must be at room temperature. Some cooks leave products like butter, eggs and flour on their kitchen bench tops overnight.

Egg yolks: Ukrainian *paska* dough is famous for being based on large quantities of egg yolks. For example, a recipe for 'Kozak's Paska' in one of the first widely published Ukrainian cookbooks, Klynovetska's *Food and Beverages in Ukraine* (1913) mentions 50 egg yolks per 6 cups of flour. Interestingly, many old recipes use cup measurements instead of measuring egg yolks in numbers. Furthermore, some also advise rubbing the egg yolks through a sieve before adding them to the dough.

Raisins: Some *paska* recipes call for raisins or other dried fruits or berries, which are usually soaked in hot water or steeped in alcohol, before being added to the dough. This allows the fruits to soften and plump up. After steeping, some advise coating the fruits in flour before adding them to the dough. This will ensure that the fruits will stay spread throughout the *paska* and will not sink to the bottom. If you prefer not to soak the dried fruits, rinse them or sprinkle with water to make the flour stick.

Yeast: Make sure that yeast is fresh. Otherwise it may have an unpleasant aroma and the dough will fail to rise. Use warm liquid to activate the yeast.

Adding boiling or hot liquid: If the recipe asks for the boiling liquid to be added to the flour, add it gradually while continually stirring the

mixture. Make sure that the mixture cools down to room temperature prior to adding the eggs or yeast mixture (starter) to it.

Flour and dough consistency: The flour should be dry and sifted. Notwithstanding that *paska* recipes indicate the amount of flour to be used, this amount can be slightly changed, if needed. The quality, level of dryness and type of flour – all these aspects have an impact on how much flour should be used to achieve the required dough consistency. Most of the *paska* recipes require dough to be soft and of medium density. The dough that is too runny will result in the *pasky* collapsing, whereas *pasky* made from thick dough will be heavy and tough.

Dough rising and kneading: The *paska* dough is customarily kneaded for a long time. An old saying was that the *paska* dough should be punched three hundred times so that guests would give three hundred praises to the *paska*. Other archaic beliefs suggest to recite two prayers, 'The Lord's Prayer' and 'The Hail Mary' twelve times by twelve (144 times) while kneading the *paska* dough. They say that the time to finish kneading *paska* dough is when you can cut it with a knife and no dough becomes stuck to it. Also, some believe that the *paska* dough should rise at least three times. The whole process of dough making should be conducted in a warm and draft-free room.

Paska dough decorations: If you choose to form some traditional dough decorations for your *paska*, there is no need to then cover your *paska* with frosting. You can use the same dough for decoration that you use for *paska*. When the dough is ready to be put in the moulds, put aside enough of it to form some ornaments. Add a little bit of flour to this dough to assure that it does not rise as much. The *paska's* decorations include figures of crosses, leaves, nets, birds and others.

Baking paska: It is best to avoid opening the oven door for at least the first 15 minutes during the *paska* baking to make sure that *paska* rises properly.

A little trick that was used by cooks in the past to make sure that *paska* rises evenly, was to stick a thin twig (a skewer will suit the purpose perfectly) in the middle of the dough. The *paska* then was baked in the oven together with the twig. When the *paska* was done baking the twig was removed. It was also used as a test to show whether the *paska* was cooked through. If the removed twig had no dough stuck to it the *paska* was ready. However the cooks who considered themselves to be the masters in the field, or observed the beliefs related to the baking of *paska* (see 'Paska – the Specialty Bread for Ukrainian Easter' on page 13) would not stoop to such tricks.

Cooling paska: The taller the *paska*, the better the chance that it might collapse when removed from a mould. One of the methods used in the past to prevent *paska* from collapsing involved a tea towel. First, the *paska* was to slightly cool in the mould. Then it was carefully placed on its side on a tea towel and rolled, lifting the ends of the towel in turns, until the *paska* cooled down. After that the *paska* could be placed upright.

Whichever way you chose to cool your *paska*, either turning to an old method and manoeuvring your *paska* with a towel or simply using a rack, make sure not to leave the bottom of the *paska* hot for too long, as it may go soft and mushy.

Improvised cheese paska mould: If you do not have a special mould to shape a cheese *paska*, you can adapt a plastic bottle for this purpose, for example a 2-litre mineral water bottle. Cut off its bottom and make a few tiny holes in its base to allow excess liquid from the cheese to escape.

Egg wash: If you choose to brush your *paska* with egg wash, make sure you brush only the top of the *paska*. Avoid brushing its sides or attaching the dough to the mould, as in both cases it would prevent the *paska* from rising.

Glaze or frosting: If you are using glaze or frosting to decorate your *paska*, the *paska* must be completely cooled before the glaze or frosting is spread.

White Glaze for Pasky

2 egg whites
250 g icing sugar
A pinch of salt

Season the egg whites with a pinch of salt and beat until stiff. Gradually add the icing sugar, continuing beating the mixture. When the pasky are cooled after baking, spread the glaze on top.

Lemon Glaze for Pasky

3 egg whites
250 g icing sugar
½ cup potato flour
1 teaspoon lemon juice

Combine all the ingredients and beat until the mixture is smooth and thick. When the pasky have cooled after baking, spread the glaze on top.

Tulle Baba

500 g flour
14 g yeast
1 cup cream
1 cup sugar
10 egg yolks, plus 1 egg yolk for brushing (optional)
¼ teaspoon salt
100 g butter, softened

Making starter: Dissolve the yeast in lukewarm cream. Combine with 1 tablespoon of sugar and 1 cup of flour. Leave for about 2 hours in a warm place to rise.

Making dough: Add the rest of the sugar and salt to the egg yolks and beat until the mixture is smooth and pale yellow. Add butter and beat until smooth. Make a well in the centre of remaining flour and add the starter and egg yolk mixture. Mix well and knead the dough. Leave it in a warm place for about 30–40 minutes to rise, then knead the dough again.

Baking baba: Set aside a little piece of dough to make some baba decorations. Place the dough into greased and floured moulds, filling to half their height. Make and arrange the decorations on top. Let the dough rise to about ¾ the height of the moulds. Optionally, brush with an egg yolk mixed with 1 teaspoon of water. Bake in a preheated oven at 150°C for about 50–60 minutes.

Golden Paska

Starter:
1½ cup milk, plus ¼ cup milk for yeast mixture
½ cup flour
¾ cup sugar, plus 1 tablespoon for yeast mixture
14 g yeast
6 egg yolks

Dough:
500 g flour
50 g butter, melted and lukewarm
¼ cup oil
½ cup mixed candied peel
¼ teaspoon cinnamon
1 egg yolk for brushing (optional)

Making starter: In a small saucepan, gradually add milk to the flour, stirring constantly. Bring to the boil on a very low heat, continuing stirring. Let the thickened milk cool to room temperature.

While the thickened milk is cooling make the yeast mixture, as it will need about 15 minutes to rise. In a small bowl dissolve 1 tablespoon of sugar and yeast in ¼ cup of lukewarm milk.

In a separate bowl, add the sugar to the egg yolks and beat until the mixture is smooth and pale yellow.

Combine the three mixtures. Leave for about 35–45 minutes in a warm place to rise.

Making dough: Cover the mixed candied peel with boiling water for about 10–15 minutes then strain.

Place the flour in a mound and make a well in the centre. Pour in the starter, butter and oil and add candied peel and cinnamon. Knead the dough until smooth. Cover the bowl with plastic wrap and leave in a warm place to rise for about 45–60 minutes.

Baking paska: Set aside a little piece of dough to make some paska decorations. Place the dough into greased and floured moulds, filling to half their height. Make and arrange the decorations on top. Let the dough rise to about ¾ the height of the moulds. Optionally, brush with an egg yolk mixed with 1 teaspoon of water. Bake in a preheated oven at 150°C for about 50–60 minutes.

Saffron Paska

Starter:
1 cup flour
1 tablespoon sugar
14 g yeast
½ cup butter, melted and lukewarm
1½ cups cooking cream
1 egg

Dough:
400 g flour
2 teaspoons saffron threads
2 tablespoons milk
1 cup sugar
8 egg yolks, plus 1 egg yolk for brushing (optional)

Making starter: Combine flour, sugar and yeast. In a separate bowl mix butter, cream and egg and then gradually add to flour mixture. Let the starter rise in a warm place for about 15–20 minutes.

Making dough: Soak saffron in 2 tablespoons of warm milk for 2–3 minutes.

Add the sugar to the egg yolks and beat until the mixture is smooth and pale yellow.

Place the flour in a mound and make a well in the centre. Pour in the starter, egg yolk mixture and saffron. Knead the dough until smooth. Cover the bowl with plastic wrap and leave in a warm place to rise for about 45–60 minutes.

Knead and let the dough rise for the second time.

Baking paska: Set aside a little bit of dough to make some paska decorations. Place the dough into greased and floured moulds, filling to half their height. Make and arrange the decorations on top. Let the dough rise to about ¾ the height of the moulds. Optionally, brush with an egg yolk mixed with 1 teaspoon of water. Bake in a preheated oven at 150°C for about 50–60 minutes.

Podillia Paska

Steeped fruit:

½ cup raisins or sultanas
¼ cup spirit (rum, liqueur, cognac or other strong spirit of your choice)
2 tablespoons flour for coating

Starter:

½ cup flour
1 cup milk, plus ½ cup milk to dissolve yeast
14 g yeast
1 teaspoon sugar

Dough:

500 g flour
12 egg yolks, plus 1 egg yolk for brushing (optional)
200 g of sugar
½ teaspoon salt
200 g butter, melted and lukewarm
2 tablespoons honey
A dash of vanilla essence
½ teaspoon ground cardamom

Steeping fruit: Place raisins or sultanas in a small bowl with the spirit of your choice and cover with a lid. Steep overnight at room temperature. Before adding the fruits to the dough, strain the liquid and coat them in flour.

Making starter: Place flour in a bowl. Bring 1 cup of milk to the boil. Gradually, add the boiling milk to the flour, stirring constantly. Mix well until smooth and silky. Let the mixture cool to room temperature.

Dissolve the yeast and sugar in ½ cup of milk and add to the mixture. Let the starter rise for about 1.5–2 hours.

Making dough: Add the sugar and salt to the egg yolks and beat until the mixture is smooth and pale yellow. Add the butter and mix well.

Place the flour in a mound and make a well in the centre. Pour in the starter, egg yolk mixture and honey. Add vanilla and cardamom to it. Knead the dough for about 30 minutes. The dough will be smooth and sticky. Cover the bowl with plastic wrap and leave in a warm place to rise for about 45–60 minutes.

Knead the dough for the second time then leave covered in a bowl to rise again.

Add steeped fruit into the dough then knead.

Baking paska: Set aside a little bit of dough to make some paska decorations. Place the dough into greased and floured moulds, filling to half their height. Make and arrange the decorations on top. Let the dough rise to about ¾ the height of the moulds. Optionally, brush with an egg yolk mixed with 1 teaspoon of water. Bake in a preheated oven at 150°C for about 50–60 minutes.

Smachna Paska

Starter:
14 g yeast
1 tablespoon sugar
½ cup milk
1/3 cup flour

Dough:
400 g flour, plus a handful of flour for coating raisins
100 g currants or sultanas
½ cup sugar
A dash of vanilla essence
1 teaspoon turmeric
½ teaspoon ground cloves
½ teaspoon ground cinnamon
½ teaspoon salt
4 egg yolks, plus 1 egg yolk for brushing (optional)
4 tablespoons sour cream
100 g butter, melted and lukewarm
1 tablespoon oil
2 tablespoons rum or cognac

Making starter: Dissolve the yeast and sugar in the milk. Gradually add to the flour, stirring constantly. Let the starter rise in a warm place for about 15–20 minutes.

Making dough: Cover currants or sultanas with boiling water for 10–15 minutes then strain.

Add the sugar, spices and salt to the egg yolks and beat until the mixture is smooth and pale yellow. Stirring constantly, gradually add sour cream, butter, oil and rum or cognac.

Place the flour in a mound and make a well in the centre. Pour in the starter and egg yolk mixture. Knead for about 25–30 minutes. Cover the bowl with plastic wrap and leave in a warm place to rise for about 45–60 minutes. Coat currants or sultanas in flour and knead into the dough. Leave covered in a bowl to rise again.

Baking paska: Set aside a little piece of dough to make some paska decorations. Place the dough into greased and floured moulds, filling to half their height. Make and arrange the decorations on top. Let the dough rise to about ¾ the height of the moulds. Optionally, brush with an egg yolk mixed with 1 teaspoon of water. Bake in a preheated oven at 150°C for about 50–60 minutes.

Almond Rye Paska

14 eggs
200 g sugar
100 g almond meal
100 g rye breadcrumbs, finely ground
½ teaspoon ground cloves
½ teaspoon ground cinnamon
½ teaspoon ground star anise

Separate the egg yolks from the egg whites into two bowls. Add the sugar to the egg yolks and beat until the mixture is smooth and pale yellow. Mix almond meal, rye breadcrumbs and spices. Gradually add to the egg yolk mixture, stirring it in gently. Beat the egg whites until they are stiff, then fold into the almond and rye breadcrumb mixture.

Place the batter into greased and floured moulds. Bake in a preheated oven at 170–180°C for about 35–45 minutes, or until ready.

Rye Paska

10 eggs
¾ cup sugar
100 g rye breadcrumbs, finely ground
1 tablespoon semolina
½ teaspoon ground cloves
½ teaspoon ground cinnamon
Zest of 1 lemon, finely grated

Separate the egg yolks from the egg whites into two bowls. Add the sugar to the egg yolks and beat until the mixture is smooth and pale yellow. Mix rye breadcrumbs, semolina, spices and lemon zest. Gradually add to the egg yolk mixture, stirring it in gently. Beat the egg whites until they are stiff, then fold into the rye breadcrumb mixture.

Place the batter into greased and floured moulds. Bake in a preheated oven at 170–180°C for about 35–45 minutes, or until ready.

About Cheese Pasky

Cheese *pasky* might not be as popular as *pasky* based on wheat flour, nonetheless, they are popular enough to join the traditional attributes of the Ukrainian Easter. Aficionados use special moulds to make cheese *paska*. The moulds are usually in the form of a pyramid without a top, a figure known in geometry as frustum. The important element of these moulds is tiny openings that allow the extra liquid from the cheese to escape, letting the cheese *paska* achieve the desired texture. The carvings inside the moulds create an ornament on top and sides of the *paska* as well as the crosses and letters 'XB' ('Christ is Risen'). Cheese *paska* is not the only cheese product featured at Easter. For instance, in Western Ukraine, it is customary to make cheese figurines especially in the form of horses for Easter (syrni konyky; Engl., 'cheese horses'). Kosiv village is famous for this craft.

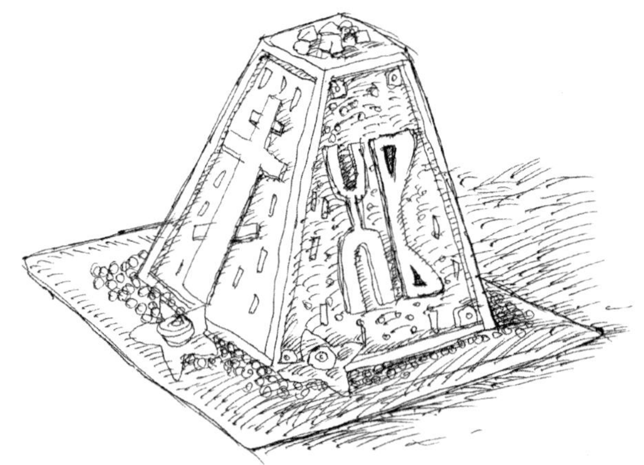

Velykden Cheese Paska

500 g cheese (syr or quark)
3 egg yolks
½ cup sour cream
100 g butter, softened
¼ cup candied orange peel
¼ cup raisins
½ cup icing sugar
1–2 drops vanilla extract

Rub the cheese through a sieve, or cream it using a blender or food processor.

Add the sugar to the egg yolks and beat until the mixture is smooth and pale yellow. Add sour cream and mix thoroughly. Put the bowl containing the mixture on a water bath or bain-marie (place the bowl into a larger pan containing water). Simmer, occasionally stirring, for 5–7 minutes or until the mixture thickens. Remove from the heat and let it cool.

Mix all the ingredients. Place into a mould with small holes in its bottom, lined with two or three layers of cheesecloth. Put a weight on top to help drain the extra liquid. Leave in a refrigerator overnight.

Prune Cheese Paska

400 g cheese (syr or quark)
5–6 prunes, pitted
½ cup cream
50 g butter, softened
½ cup icing sugar

Cover prunes with boiling water for about 15 minutes or until tender. Strain off as much liquid as possible then chop the prunes finely. Whip the cream. Mix butter with icing sugar.

Rub the cheese through a sieve, or cream it using a food processor. Add prunes, cream and butter. Mix well. Place into a mould with small holes in its bottom, lined with two or three layers of cheesecloth. Put a weight on top to help drain the extra liquid. Leave in a refrigerator overnight.

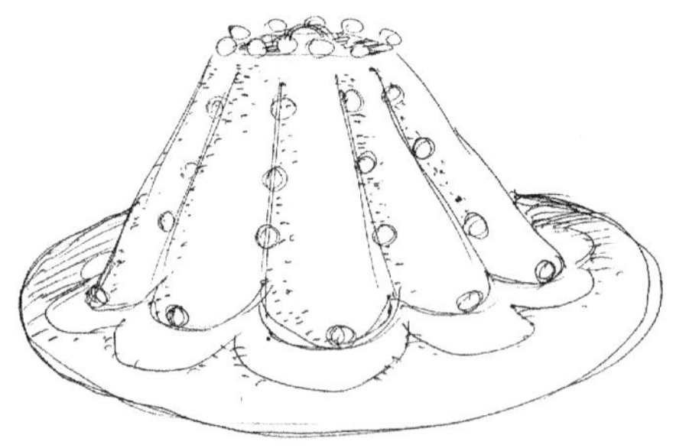

Mock Cheese Paska

6 eggs
2 cups sour cream
2 cups milk
200 g butter, softened
1 cup icing sugar

Making egg and milk mixture: Beat the eggs lightly then combine with sour cream and milk. In a small saucepan bring the mixture to the boil, stirring constantly. Cook on a very low heat for about a minute. Cool to room temperature then move into a colander lined with two or three layers of cheesecloth. Leave for 5–6 hours to strain away extra liquid.

Making mock cheese: Beat the softened butter with the icing sugar until light and creamy. Continue beating it, gradually adding the egg and milk mixture one tablespoon at a time. Place the mixture into a mould covered with plastic wrap (plastic wrap will help to remove the paska more easily when it sets). Refrigerate for 3–4 hours, or until it has set. Serve chilled.

Borshch and Soup

Borshch or soups may not be commonly associated with the Easter table, but in some regions of Ukraine it is a customary Easter dish. In Verkhovyna, for example, where a popular *borshch* recipe is based on pickled white beets (fodder beets), they serve it differently for Easter, marking the occasion with a red *borshch* (based on red beetroot). One such recipe, 'Velykden Borshch', is presented in this chapter.

Like almost all the foods that are served for Easter, the *borshch* cooked for this occasion is abundant with flavoursome ingredients. These may include smoked *buzhenyna*, *kovbasa*, sour cream, eggs as a garnish for green *borshch* and some not-so-traditional ingredients, like olives. One recipe for green *borshch* is also included. Green *borshch* is usually based on sorrel or spinach or some other leafy vegetables and herbs that appear in spring and early in summer in Ukraine.

Solianka is a soup with the star ingredient of pickled or marinated gherkins. In this book, solianka is represented by the recipe for 'Panska Solianka'. Derived from 'pan' (Engl., 'sir' or 'landlord') 'panska', has the connotation of something that is available or fitted to a well-to-do person.

The *borshch* and soup recipes that are offered here suit the Easter menu perfectly. Like most of the other dishes served for Easter celebrations they are cooked a day before the event and are served reheated, after having their flavours infused overnight.

Velykden green borshch and boryshnyk

Velykden Green Borshch

2–3 potatoes, peeled and cubed
2 litres ham stock (see'Ham Stock' on page 100)
Ham removed from the bone used to make stock
1 bunch sorrel or spinach or to taste
½ cup spring onion, finely chopped
Salt and ground black pepper to taste
Butter for frying

Garnish:
Sour cream
½ hard-boiled egg per portion
Chopped dill or parsley

Place potatoes in boiling stock and simmer for about 20 minutes or until cooked.

Sauté sorrel or spinach and onion in preheated butter for about 1 minute. Add pieces of ham and sautéed vegetables to the stock and season with salt and pepper to taste. Simmer for another minute and remove from the heat.

Serve with a generous dollop of sour cream, half an egg, dill or parsley.

Velykden Borshch

3 cups pickled beetroot with kvas (see 'Pickled Beetroot and Kvas' on page 101)
2 litres ham stock (see 'Ham Stock' on page 100)
Ham removed from the bone used to make stock
1 carrot, peeled and finely grated
1 onion, peeled and finely chopped
2 cloves garlic, peeled and crushed
1 teaspoon dried thyme
Salt and ground black pepper to taste
Oil and butter for frying
Sour cream and finely chopped parsley for garnish

Add julienned pickled beetroot with kvas to the simmering ham stock and bring to the boil. Reduce heat and simmer for about 20 minutes.

Sauté carrot and onion in preheated oil and butter for about 3–4 minutes.

Add pieces of ham, sautéed vegetables, garlic and thyme to the stock. Season with salt and pepper and simmer for 2–3 minutes.

Remove from heat and let the borshch rest for at least 20 minutes before serving. Serve hot, garnished with sour cream and parsley.

Panska Solianka

Meat and stock:

300–400 g pork
300–400 g lamb
1 onion, peeled
1 carrot, peeled and coarsely chopped
1 bay leaf
3–4 black peppercorns
5–6 allspice berries
Salt to taste

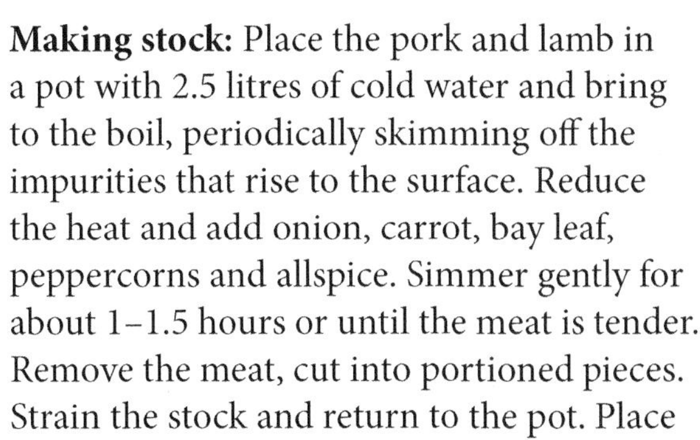

Solianka:

2 potatoes, peeled and cubed
1 onion, peeled and finely chopped
1 carrot, peeled and coarsely grated
3–4 pickled gherkins, peeled and coarsely grated
¼ cup olives, pitted and sliced
1 veal tongue, cooked and sliced (see 'Simmered Tongue' on page 99)
200 g ham or smoked kovbasa, sliced
2 tablespoons tomato paste
Salt, sugar and ground back pepper to taste
Butter for frying
Sour cream, chopped dill or parsley for garnish

Making stock: Place the pork and lamb in a pot with 2.5 litres of cold water and bring to the boil, periodically skimming off the impurities that rise to the surface. Reduce the heat and add onion, carrot, bay leaf, peppercorns and allspice. Simmer gently for about 1–1.5 hours or until the meat is tender. Remove the meat, cut into portioned pieces. Strain the stock and return to the pot. Place the meat back into the stock.

Making solianka: Bring the stock back to boil. Add potatoes and simmer for about 10–15 minutes.

Sauté onion and carrot in butter for 3–4 minutes, add gherkins, olives, tongue and ham or kovbasa and sauté for another 2 minutes. Mix in tomato paste and, stirring constantly, cook for about a minute. Season with salt, sugar and pepper. Add 1 cup of stock, mix thoroughly and bring to the boil.

Add the sautéed mixture to the stock. Simmer for about 10 minutes. Remove from the heat and let it stand for at least 25–30 minutes.

Serve hot, garnished with sour cream and chopped dill or parsley.

Eggs and Cheese

During Great Lent, which lasts almost six weeks prior to Easter Sunday, the faithful abstain from eggs and cheese, since these are animal by-products and, as such, they are not allowed to be consumed during this time. However, with Easter's arrival these products become the most popular ingredients to cook with.

In the past, the traditional *krashanky* were made in dozens. Nowadays, fewer eggs are cooked for the occasion, but even so, no household goes without them. A few of these hard-boiled and dyed eggs are then blessed in church together with cheese and some other items during the special Resurrection Service (see 'Velykden Koshyk – the Easter Basket' on page 46). The blessed *krashanky* together with *paska* are the first foods consumed during *roszhovyny*. The remaining *krashanky* are then served at subsequent meals. A few recipes in this chapter suggest some variations for serving *krashanky*.

Cheese is used to make both savoury and sweet Easter dishes. Some dishes use a tiny amount of cheese, see for example 'Cheese Stuffing' on page 43 for 'Stuffed Eggs'. Other dishes use cheese as their basis and incorporate additional ingredients to add some distinct flavour, see for example, cheese *paska* recipes (see 'Paska, Baba or Babka – Velykden Bread' on page 11). This chapter offers a few savoury cheese dishes.

The Magical Dyed Egg – Krashanka

Krashanky, *pysanky*, and other types of decorated eggs were known to the ancient Ukrainians during pre-Christian times and were made in celebration of the Sun and spring. These ritual eggs were enfolded by such irresistible mystery and were attributed so many magic powers that no prohibitions – under any religion or any political regime – could ever get rid of this symbol of the sun and new life. With the arrival of Christianity, *pysanky* and *krashanky* were smoothly amalgamated into the celebration of Easter. However, despite becoming a part of the Christian tradition, they firmly retained their pre-Christian attributes and rituals, especially the beliefs that people invested in them.

Pysanky are the Easter eggs that are perhaps more elegant than *krashanky* and decorated with intricate multi-coloured ancient designs and symbols. As such, they attracted more attention from ethnographers and other experts in the field. Many good monographs have been written on *pysanky*, some of which are available in English. Luba Petrusha, a contemporary advocate of Ukrainian traditions, has compiled a thorough bibliography on *pysanky*, which is available on her website: www.pysanky.info.

Although the *krashanka* was not as fortunate as *pysanka* in regards to having its story told, there is still enough information to get an idea of what *krashanka* signifies. Following are some examples of the important role that was assigned to a blessed *krashanka* in the Ukrainian culture.

There used to be a lovely custom in Ukraine, when after the Easter Vigil people gifted each other with *krashanky* or *pysanky*, while exchanging Easter greetings. The custom survived only in a few places, such as Verkhovyna. It was believed that the first *krashanka* or *pysanka* that was received during such an exchange of Easter greetings possessed special powers. Therefore, it was kept in a safe place as a protection from the evil eye or hex. Another widespread belief was that if, during a fire, such an egg was thrown into the fire or over the burning building, the fire will cease.

Either because the word *krashanka* is related to the word 'krasa' (Engl., 'beauty'), or because the most popular colour for *krashanky* was red, the colour associated with healthy, rosy cheeks, there is a ritual in Ukraine to 'wash one's face with *krashanka*'. It is believed that you will be good looking and healthy if you follow this ritual: one of the oldest members of the family puts two or more *krashanky*, most often dyed red, in a bowl with water. Then each member of the family in turn puts some water on their faces with their hands. Any young woman of the family who wished to get married soon, would have the first turn at washing her face and then would take one *krashanka* for herself.

There was a tradition of putting *krashanky* on a table in a bowl with grass, or to be more precise with wheatgrass. The number of the *krashanky* in the bowl equalled the number of departed family members. Having these *krashanky* in the house was as though their souls were joining the family for Easter celebrations. In order to have a bowl with wheatgrass for Easter, you need to start about two weeks beforehand. In a thin layer place some soil in a bowl then plant the wheat seeds. Store in a warm place with plenty of light and keep the soil moist. By Easter the bottom of the bowl will be covered in a delicate wheatgrass carpet.

A beautiful but sad ritual was performed by mothers who did not know of their children's whereabouts. They would wrap three *krashanky* and a piece of *paska* in a *rushnyk* then put this parcel into a safe place and with a dried twig of oregano on it. (One of several folk names for oregano in Ukrainian is 'materynka', a noun derived from word 'matir' (Engl., 'mother'). In Ukrainian tradition the plant is a symbol of mother's love.) This symbolic sacrifice was later given to the poor, who would then pray for the lost child.

The power of *krashanka* was so great, that even its leftover eggshell had the ability to protect. Together with other blessed food leftovers, the *krashanka* eggshell was buried on the edge of the cereal field or in the garden. This eggshell was to shield the crops from storm or hail. Also, a very finely ground *krashanka* eggshell added to hens' food would ensure they have more eggs.

In the form of incense the *krashanka* eggshell could be utilised for the treatment of a sick person. The smoke of a burning eggshell was considered to have curative properties. The eggshells of blessed *krashanky* added to burning embers were used to treat a person suffering from fever, night-blindness and toothache.

If you are not planning to use the *krashanka* eggshell to protect your garden or feed your chicks, you should at least break it into the tiniest pieces. These pieces must be so small that a witch could not gather even a drop of dew with them, otherwise she could use that dew to make a cow sick.

Whatever you do, make sure that no drop of blessed *krashanka*, including its eggshell, falls on the ground and you do not step on it. Some say it is a grave sin to do so, and you may become ill as a result.

Stuffed eggs: paprika, beetroot, cheese and pashtet stuffing

Eggs with Mayonnaise

5–6 hard-boiled eggs
3 tablespoons mayonnaise (see 'Home-made Mayonnaise' on page 79)
2 tablespoons chopped spring onion
A pinch of nutmeg
Salt to taste

Mix mayonnaise with spring onion. Cut eggs into wedges and arrange on a serving dish. Drizzle the mayonnaise mixture on the top and sprinkle with nutmeg and salt to taste.

Eggs with Cold Horseradish Sauce

5–6 hard-boiled eggs
1 tablespoon grated horseradish
1 cup sour cream
1 teaspoon vinegar
Salt and sugar to taste

Mix horseradish, sour cream and vinegar. Season with salt and sugar to taste. Stir well. Cut eggs into wedges or round slices, arrange on a serving dish and drizzle with the sauce.

Eggs with Hot Horseradish Sauce

5–6 hard-boiled eggs
2–3 tablespoons butter
1 tablespoon grated horseradish
2 teaspoons flour
1 cup sour cream
2 egg yolks
1 teaspoon vinegar
Salt and sugar to taste

Melt butter in a small saucepan. Add horseradish and, stirring constantly, fry for 1–2 minutes. Sprinkle with flour and fry for another minute. Add sour cream thoroughly mixed with egg yolks, and vinegar. Season with salt and sugar to taste. Stir well, bring to the boil and then remove from the heat. Cut eggs into wedges or round slices, arrange on a serving dish and drizzle with the sauce.

Eggs in Sour Cream

5–6 hard-boiled eggs
½ cup sour cream
2–3 tablespoons cheese (syr, quark or creamed cottage cheese)
½ tablespoon chopped dill or parsley
Salt and ground black pepper to taste
Oil for greasing

Combine sour cream, cheese and dill or parsley. Season with salt to taste and mix well. Cut eggs into round slices and arrange on an oiled shallow baking dish, sprinkling with salt and pepper to taste. Bake in a preheated oven at 180°C for 10–15 minutes or until golden.

Stuffed Eggs

6 hard-boiled eggs

Peel and cut the eggs lengthways in halves. Remove the egg yolks and use them for stuffing (choose from the recipes below). Place the stuffing into the white egg halves. Serve chilled, garnished with fresh herbs.

Meat Stuffing

6 egg yolks removed from eggs cooked for stuffing
½ cup meat (any cooked meat of your choice)
1 tablespoon mayonnaise
1 tablespoon sour cream
1 teaspoon horseradish, finely grated
1 teaspoon mustard
1 tablespoon spring onion, chopped
Salt and ground black pepper to taste

You may take some of the roasted, simmered or other meat cooked for another Easter dish. Finely chop or mince the meat. Mash egg yolks with a fork and mix with the rest of the ingredients. Optionally, mince the mixture for the second time.

Pashtet Stuffing

6 egg yolks removed from eggs cooked for stuffing
½ cup pâté
1 small onion
Salt and ground black pepper to taste
Oil for frying

Sauté finely chopped onion in oil until golden. Allow it to cool. Mash egg yolks with a fork and mix with the rest of the ingredients. Alternatively, mince the mixture.

Smoked Stuffing

6 egg yolks removed from eggs cooked for stuffing
½ cup smoked ham or kovbasa, finely chopped
2 tablespoons butter, softened
Salt and ground black pepper to taste

Mash egg yolks with a fork. Combine all the ingredients together and mince using a food processor.

Beetroot Stuffing

6 egg yolks removed from eggs cooked for stuffing
1 tablespoon mayonnaise
1 tablespoon horseradish, finely grated
1 tablespoon beetroot, cooked and finely grated
Salt, sugar and ground black pepper to taste

This stuffing is convenient to make if you are also preparing Tsvikli (see 'Tsvikli' on page 71) for the occasion. In this case replace horseradish and beetroot with 2 tablespoons of Tsvikli.

Mash egg yolks with a fork and combine with the rest of the ingredients.

Cheese Stuffing

6 egg yolks removed from eggs cooked for stuffing
2 tablespoons cheese (syr, quark or creamed cottage cheese)
1 tablespoon cream or sour cream
1 clove garlic
½ teaspoon paprika
¼ teaspoon dried dill (or 1 teaspoon fresh dill, finely chopped)
Salt to taste

Mash egg yolks with a fork and thoroughly mix with the rest of the ingredients. Alternatively, mince the mixture.

Herring Stuffing

6 egg yolks removed from eggs cooked for stuffing
1 small herring fillet, chopped
1 tablespoon mayonnaise
1 teaspoon mustard
Salt and ground black pepper to taste

Mash egg yolks with a fork. Combine all the ingredients together and mince using a food processor.

Paprika Stuffing

6 egg yolks removed from eggs cooked for stuffing
½ tablespoon mayonnaise
½ tablespoon cream or sour cream
½ teaspoon paprika
½ mustard powder
½ tablespoon fresh herbs (chives, spring onion or parsley), finely chopped
Salt and ground black pepper to taste

Mash egg yolks with a fork and thoroughly mix with the rest of the ingredients. Alternatively, mince the mixture.

Melted Cheese

1 litre milk
1 kg cheese (syr, quark or creamed cottage cheese)
1 egg
½ teaspoon baking soda
Salt to taste
2 tablespoons butter
1 tablespoon cumin seeds
½ cup chopped walnuts

Bring milk to the boil. Add cheese and, stirring constantly with a wooden spoon, bring back to the boil. Reduce the heat then simmer, continuing to stir for 5–7 minutes or until lemon-coloured whey appears.

Strain the cheese through a piece of cheesecloth and let it cool. Rub through a sieve or in a food processor. Thoroughly mix with egg, baking soda and salt to taste.

Melt butter in a cast iron frying pan and add the cheese mixture. Cook on a low heat stirring for about 15–20 minutes. The mixture should be smooth and silky.

Two minutes before the end of cooking add cumin seeds and walnuts and mix thoroughly. Pour the cheese into a mould and let it cool at room temperature.

A little tip: there will be a layer of thin crust left on the frying pan from the cheese. Try to remove it while it is still hot, otherwise it will be harder to remove.

Piquant Cheese Spread

300 g cheese (syr, quark or creamed cottage cheese)
1 tablespoon oil
1–2 cloves garlic, crushed
½ cup walnuts, chopped
½ tablespoon chopped dill
1 teaspoon coriander seeds
1 teaspoon cumin seeds
Salt and ground chilli to taste

Serve with:
Bread (optional)
3–4 tomatoes (optional)
2–3 cucumbers (optional)

Combine all the ingredients. Leave in a refrigerator for 20–30 minutes. Serve chilled with bread or sliced tomatoes or cucumbers.

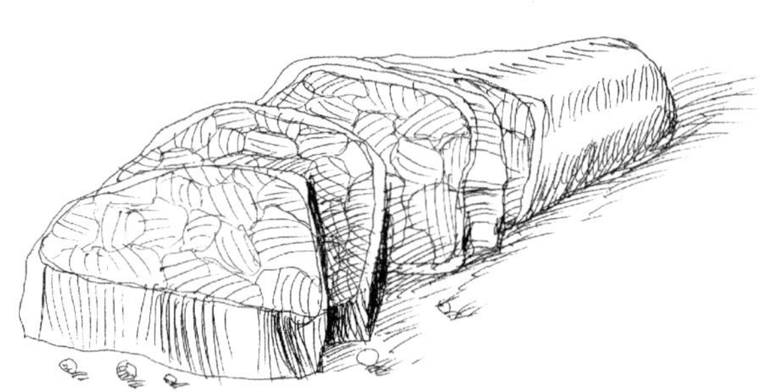

Cheese and Herring Spread

300 g cheese (syr, quark or creamed cottage cheese)
1 herring fillet
2 tablespoons sour cream
2 fresh cucumbers
1 spring onion
½ teaspoon fennel seeds

Serve with:
Rye bread (optional)

Thoroughly mix cheese, sour cream and fennel seeds. Finely chop the herring fillet. Peel, deseed and chop the cucumbers. Finely chop the spring onion. Mix everything. Serve chilled as a spread or as a side dish.

Velykden Koshyk – the Easter Basket

A bystander unfamiliar with Ukrainian Easter traditions might be surprised to see so many well-dressed people arriving at church and carrying baskets on Easter Sunday. These mysterious baskets contain delicious foods and a few other items that will be blessed by the priest at the end of Resurrection Service. On their return home, the families will consume the food to break the fast they have adhered to for the whole 40 days of the Great Lent.

The basket is covered with an embroidered cloth, often *rushnyk*. In the basket a towering, delectable-looking *paska* has a candle on its top or next to it. Some other products surround the *paska* and each of them has its own significance. The traditional and 'approved' products that are included in the basket are: *paska*, butter and *syr* (cheese); decorated eggs (*krashanky* and *pysanky*); *shynka or buzhenyna*, *salo* or *kovbasa*; horseradish and salt. The basket is decorated with branches of an evergreen plant, such as periwinkle or myrtle.

Throughout the centuries, some peculiar and out-of-place objects have also found their way into the Easter basket. In modern times these objects might include banknotes or new car keys. By adding them to the basket, the owners hope that the priest's blessing will confer financial stability or, in the second instance, prolong the car's life.

Below is a list of the most common items that Ukrainian families bless on the occasion of Easter. Following the assumption that Ukrainian Easter has its roots in the pre-Christian celebration of the resurrection of spring and the new sun, the information below touches upon the pre-Christian symbolism and folk beliefs. In the Christian church, the significance of these products is interpreted as relating to Jesus Christ, His resurrection and teachings.

Paska – Along with *krashanky* and *pysanky*, the *paska* is one of the chief items to be blessed on the occasion of Easter. *Paska* (ritual Easter bread) is a type of a modernised offering. Centuries ago the Ukrainian ancestors had a custom of baking bread at this time of year and offering it as a gift to the Sun, Earth and forefathers. Even comparatively recently, some hundred years ago, a cook baking *paska* would have chanted some ancient spells asking for health and fortune for her family in return for the bread. The *paska* is a 'modernised' offering because the ritual began prior to the use of leavening methods, when bread was usually a simple unleavened flatbread. Some believe that *paska* symbolises the sun because of its round form. For more on *paska* see 'Paska – the Specialty Bread for Ukrainian Easter' on page 13.

Eggs – The most popular types of Ukrainian Easter eggs are *pysanky* and *krashanky* (there are also *driapanky* and *krapanky*). The Easter eggs are 'a must' item in the Easter basket. Depending on the region of Ukraine, either *krashanky* or *pysanky* may prevail. The interesting detail is that in some areas of Ukraine, for example, Verkhovyna, either *krashanky* or simple hard-boiled eggs that are brought to the church for blessing are already peeled and sometimes cut in half. This way, the people believe, the eggs will be properly blessed since holy water will fall on the egg white or yolk as opposed its shell. For more on *krashanky* see 'The Magical Dyed Egg – Krashanka' on page 36. The egg, in general, and its mystifying nature often features in Ukrainian lore because life manifesting from an animate object appeared so magical to the onlooker. The egg came to symbolise life, new beginnings and nature's revival in springtime.

Candle – The presence of a candle in the Easter basket is a tiny part of the vast ritual connected with fire. According to the old tradition, on the night before Easter Sunday bonfires were lit from 'live' fire (meaning fire ignited by rubbing sticks or striking stones) in the villages and kept going all through the night preceding Easter. The Ukrainian ancestors, whose cult of the Sun was rather profound, believed fire to be a part of the Sun or its representation on Earth. Fire, like water, had cleansing powers. It protected people from evil spirits and cured ailments. The power of fire is so strong that candlelight is enough to warm the souls of the deceased relatives, who were thought to celebrate their Easter around the same time of year as the living celebrated Easter.

Butter and **syr** (cheese) – The faithful abstain from these products, among others, during the long weeks of the Great Lent that precedes Easter. Butter and *syr* also fell into a category of foods that were not easily affordable, which follows the theory that the foods selected for the church blessing are the remnants of the prehistoric offerings, where only the best was sacrificed to the higher power. An interesting observation was made by Mykola Sumtsov, who believed that while the Celts and Germanic peoples did not have much use for cheese, the Slavs have used it since ancient times; and it might have even preceded bread, being a product of pastoralism, one of the oldest traits of the Proto-Indo-Europeans.

Now firmly established as components of the Easter basket, often a cross is carved on the piece of butter or cheese to be blessed.

Pork – Upon seeing a picture of a roasted piglet with a horseradish in its mouth any Ukrainian would know that the dish was cooked on the occasion of Easter. The Ukrainian ethnographer Oleksa Voropaj offered an interesting theory as to why Ukrainians would prepare a roasted piglet for Easter. Apparently, the Ukrainian pre-Christian ancestors borrowed the custom of roasting a pig for their celebration of Sun from the Goths, who also used it as a sacrifice to the Sun. With time the roasted piglet became a popular item in the Easter basket, especially among those who could afford it. In modern times the whole piglet was replaced by various other pork dishes, including *salo*, *shynka* or *buzhenyna* and *kovbasa*. According to Ukrainian folk beliefs, blessed objects acquire magic powers, and that includes blessed *salo*. The Ukrainian villagers used to believe that one of the best ways to make sure that you get plentiful and good quality sour cream is to smear the jugs, in which the sour cream is made, with a piece of blessed *salo*.

Horseradish – The horseradish plant is a symbol of strength and health. Like some other items in the Easter basket, the blessed horseradish was used in treatment of ailments – for example, nausea. According to an old

Blessing of pasky. Fr. Michael Smolynec, Pokrova UOC, Sydney, Australia

legend the horseradish was once a poisonous plant. The enemies of Jesus wanted to kill him and gave him some of the horseradish root to eat. However, Jesus did not die. He then told his followers to eat the horseradish and this would assure that they stayed healthy and strong.

Salt – In the past, salt was not as easily available or as affordable as it is nowadays. Consequently, it became a symbol of abundance and completeness. Blessed salt was considered to be a multi-purpose agent against evil. Simply sprinkling the blessed salt along a doorway could ensure that no person with bad intentions would be able to enter the house. Also, salt had curative powers. In some villages a preparation ritual for Easter celebrations involved 'baking' salt in the oven. The ritual took place on Maundy Thursday. The woman of the house put some salt in a cloth and wrapped it into a bundle. The bundle was carefully placed into a hot corner of the oven with the accompaniment of certain spells. As soon as the cloth smouldered, it was time to take the salt bundle from the oven. On Easter Sunday, during *rozhovyny*, the salt was placed on a loaf of bread and then beneath icons. This salt was later used to treat unwell cattle, if required.

Periwinkle, **myrtle** or **buxus** – In Ukrainian culture, these evergreen plants symbolise immortality and eternal life. In relation to Easter, the plants reflect the spirit of the feast itself: in pre-Christian tradition they symbolised the never-dying essence of nature as well as the victory of spring's sun, light and warmth over the winter's coldness and darkness; in Christianity they represent the resurrection of Jesus Christ. The branches of the plants were either put together with other objects in the basket, or used as basket decorations. Interestingly, the custom in some villages was to decorate an Easter roasted piglet with a periwinkle wreath.

Throughout the centuries, items that Ukrainians blessed for Easter included some with a tenuous connection to the sublime meaning of the festival's celebrations. Despite the church's continuing disapproval these items stubbornly appeared in the church or churchyard for one of the most important services of the Christian year. The reason for that is that people put much trust into blessed items and conferred supernatural powers on them. Blessed items were deemed to be very useful within the household, even for curing a disease or removing a curse. Following are some examples of the more conventional blessed items.

Millet – When blessed, millet was used together with salt to treat fever. Here is a summary of a very old ritual: a sufferer takes the blessed millet with salt; throws the mixture over his head or shoulder with the words: 'There are seventy-seven of you, aunties. I brought bread and salt for you all."

Poppy seeds – Poppy seeds have a strong and extensive symbolism in Ukrainian folklore and culture and, among other things, they symbolise fertility. At Easter the blessed poppy seeds were given to poultry and other farm animals, in the belief that they would multiply better.

Chillies – In some areas people believed that adding a little of the blessed chilli to food would prevent illness. Interestingly, the same ritual applied to the feeding of turkey chicks, as well.

Incense – Smoking incense was used around someone who was affected by illness or witchcraft. It was believed that the ground eggshell of *krashanky* had the same powers as blessed incense and on occasions a mixture of both was used.

Bar (wooden) – A blessed wooden bar was of great assistance if you owned a cow. The bar was used to treat the cow's udder if it was unwell and to protect it from witches who sucked the cow's milk at night, making the cow ill.

Needles – It was believed that blessed needles were a sure cure for night-blindness. The sufferer must look through the needle hole into the distance and then throw the needle away.

Knife – In addition to its use for treating illnesses or removing a curse, a blessed knife also had the power to find a fern flower. Those who are familiar with Ukrainian folklore know that it is a breeze to discover a buried treasure if you have a fern flower. In order to see this mysterious blossom, you need the tablecloth in which you wrapped your food to take to church to be blessed for Easter. The tablecloth needs to have been used for this purpose for seven years in a row and not have been washed in the meantime. You also need a knife blessed at Easter Vigil, a plate and a Bible. With these items, in a forest at midnight on the eve of Green Week one is able to see how fern flower blossoms.

The range of products and items blessed on the occasion of Easter underlines how tightly pre-Christian traditions were intertwined with the Christian dogmas. It also illustrates the matters of most importance to the people throughout the centuries: their health and means of living, including their household, livestock and crops, which all depended on good weather and the higher power that controlled it.

Meats

The Ukrainians prepare a great variety of meat dishes for Easter: smoked and roasted *kovbasa, shynka* or *buzhenyna, kholodets, salo, saltseson* and many others. Some of the dishes, like a piece of *kovbasa, shynka* or *buzhenyna* and *salo* are included in the Easter basket to be blessed at the Resurrection Service (see 'Velykden Koshyk – the Easter Basket' on page 46).

There also used to be a tradition of roasting a whole piglet for the occasion. The roasted piglet was decorated with a couple of other traditional items from the Easter basket: a horseradish, which was placed into its mouth; and occasionally periwinkle, which was twined into a wreath and placed on its head. Although the typical Ukrainian Easter menu no longer features the roasted piglet, there is no lack of delicious meat dishes, among which pork is the most popular ingredient. Veal or beef dishes and, more rarely, lamb are also present.

Traditionally, poultry was not commonly cooked for Easter. Some think that this custom relates to the important association of eggs with Easter, which makes the killing of poultry seem inappropriate.

Rye poliadvytsia, cherry silverside, shynka in kvas

Shynka in Kvas

2 kg piece of pork neck or loin
4–5 cloves garlic
Salt and ground black pepper to taste
Oil and butter for frying

Marinade:

1 litre (4 cups) kvas
3 tablespoons vinegar
2 onions, peeled and sliced in rings
5 sprigs parsley
2 bay leaves
1 teaspoon dried mint
1 teaspoon whole black peppercorns
1 teaspoon allspice berries
1 tablespoon salt
2 teaspoons sugar

Marinating: Mix together all the ingredients and bring to the boil. Let the mixture cool to room temperature.

While the mixture is cooling, thoroughly rub the pork with salt and pepper. Place the pork into a large container and pour the marinade over it. Close the container and leave it in the refrigerator for about 48 hours.

Roasting: After the pork has been marinated, remove it from the container and reserve the marinade.

Peel and quarter the garlic cloves. Make thin and deep incisions in the pork piece and insert the garlic into the incisions.

Heat some oil and butter in a frying pan and fry the pork piece on each side or until golden brown to seal in the juices. Place it on a roasting tray and pour the oil and butter from the frying pan, as well as some of the reserved marinade, over the pork. Cover the tray with a lid or aluminium foil. Put the roasting tray in a preheated oven at 180°C for 1–1.5 hours or until cooked to your liking. About 10–15 minutes prior to removing the pork from the oven, add the onion rings from the marinade and continue roasting uncovered.

Let the roasted pork rest for about 10 minutes. Serve hot or cold.

Kholodets

3 kg pig's feet
1½ kg pork shanks
2 carrots
2 root parsley
3 onions
2–3 bay leaves
12 whole black peppercorns
6–7 whole allspice berries
5–6 cloves garlic
Salt to taste

Cover the pig's feet and the shanks with cold water and soak for 3–4 hours. Discard the water.

Place the pig's feet and shanks into a large pot and cover with cold water. Bring to the boil, periodically skimming off the impurities that rise to the surface. Add vegetables (except garlic), spices and a little salt. Bring to the boil, reduce the heat and simmer on a very low heat for 3–4 hours until the meat is easily removed from the bones. Turn off the heat and let the stock sit for about 15 minutes to allow the fat to rise to the top. Skim off all the fat and strain the stock into another pot.

Season the stock with crushed garlic and salt to taste. Let it stand for another 15 minutes. Strain the stock again.

Slice or shred meat into small pieces and place into serving dishes. Pour over the stock. Place the dishes in the refrigerator for the kholodets to set. Serve with mustard or horseradish sauces or relishes.

About Kholodets

A Ukrainian classic, *kholodets* has been a very popular dish for centuries. Simply described, *kholodets* is meat in aspic. Ukrainian connoisseurs strongly believe that real *kholodets* should be made without adding manufactured gelatine. The jellied texture of the dish in this recipe for pork *kholodets*, is achieved by using the pig's feet. The pig's feet for this purpose should be lightly broiled on all sides, as it gives that lovely smoky flavour to the dish. Buy the pig's feet whole (as opposed to split). Thoroughly rinse them, then pat dry. Broil the pig's feet and avoid scorching them. Rinse again, scraping off all the impurities. Only then cut the feet lengthways. Otherwise, simply ask your butcher to cut the pigs' feet for you.

Importantly, *kholodets* should be simmered on a very low heat. Rapid boiling will ruin the clarity of the broth. Also, *kholodets* is supposed to be cooked for several hours and more rapid cooking means that more stock than necessary would evaporate.

Dolyna Buzhenyna

1½–2 kg piece of pork loin
Oil for roasting
Kitchen string (optional)

Marinating mixture:

1½ tablespoons salt or to taste
1 teaspoon ground black pepper
1 tablespoon caraway seeds
½ tablespoon thyme
½ tablespoon marjoram
½ tablespoon oregano
½ tablespoon mustard seeds
1 tablespoon ready mustard
1 tablespoon honey
2 tablespoons butter, softened

Marinating: Thoroughly rub the pork loin with salt and pepper. Wrap it in plastic wrap and refrigerate for about 30–40 minutes.

Combine the rest of the ingredients and massage the mixture into the meat. Wrap the pork loin in plastic wrap again and leave in the refrigerator overnight.

Roasting: Optionally, tie the pork with a kitchen string to help it keep its form.

Place the pork on an oiled roasting tray and put in a preheated oven at 220°C for 25–30 minutes then reduce to 160°C and continue to cook for about 1 hour or until cooked to your liking. The meat is cooked if the juices run clear (not pink) when you pierce the thickest part of the meat with a skewer.

Let the roasted pork rest for about 15 minutes before serving. Serve hot or cold.

Shynka with Sour Cream

1½ kg piece of pork neck or loin
Salt and ground black pepper to taste
Oil and butter (or lard) for frying

Marinade:
2 litres (8 cups) water
2 cups white vinegar (or apple cider vinegar)
1 tablespoon salt
2 tablespoons sugar
1 onion, whole
2–3 bay leaves
6–8 juniper berries
4–6 allspice berries
4–5 cloves
1 teaspoon black peppercorns

Sauce:
2 tablespoons butter
1 tablespoon flour
½ cup sour cream
Salt to taste

Marinating: Mix together all the ingredients, except for the vinegar, and bring the mixture to the boil. Reduce the heat then simmer for about 10 minutes. Add vinegar and bring back to the boil. Remove from heat. Let the marinade cool and discard the onion.

While the mixture is cooling, thoroughly rub the pork with salt and pepper. Place the pork into a large container and pour the marinade over it. Close the container and leave it in a refrigerator for about 2–3 days.

Roasting: After the pork has been marinated, remove it from the container. Reserve the marinade. Pat dry the meat with a paper towel. Heat some oil and butter or lard in a frying pan and fry each side of the pork piece until golden brown to seal in the juices. Place the pork on a roasting tray and pour the oil and butter from the frying pan, as well as some of the reserved marinade, over the pork. Put the roasting tray in a preheated oven at 180°C for about 1.5 hours or until cooked. The meat is cooked if the juices run clear (not pink) when you pierce the thickest part of the meat with a skewer. About 10–15 minutes prior to removing the pork from the oven, pour the sauce over the pork.

Sauce: In a frying pan lightly brown the flour in the butter. Gradually add sour cream and the mixture of meat juices and marinade from the roasting tray, stirring the sauce constantly. Simmer for about 1 minute.

Let the roasted pork rest for about 15 minutes before serving. Serve hot or cold.

Spicy Pork Belly Roll

2–2½ kg pork belly (thin and wide square piece)
5 cloves garlic, peeled and crushed
1 onion, peeled and thinly grated
1 teaspoon dried chilli flakes
1 tablespoon thyme leaves
1 teaspoon ground cloves
½ teaspoon black pepper
2 teaspoons salt

Stock:
1 onion
3 bay leaves
5 whole allspice berries
6–7 whole black peppercorns
Salt and pepper to taste

Kitchen string for tying pork belly roll

Rinse and pat dry the piece of pork belly. Squeeze juice from grated onion through a cheesecloth or fine sieve and combine with the rest of the herbs and spices. Place the pork belly skin down on a workbench and thoroughly rub the mixture into the meat. Roll the pork belly and secure it with string. Wrap the roll in plastic wrap and refrigerate for about 3–4 hours. Just before cooking it allow the meat to come to room temperature.

Place the roll into a large saucepan and cover with water. Bring to the boil, periodically skimming off the impurities that rise to the surface.

Add onion, bay leaves, allspice, peppercorns and season with salt and pepper. Simmer on a very low heat with a slightly open lid for 3–3.5 hours or until cooked through. Let the meat cool in the stock. Strain the stock (you can use the stock for another dish). Wrap the pork belly roll in plastic wrap and leave refrigerated overnight. Remove the string from the roll before serving. Serve chilled and sliced.

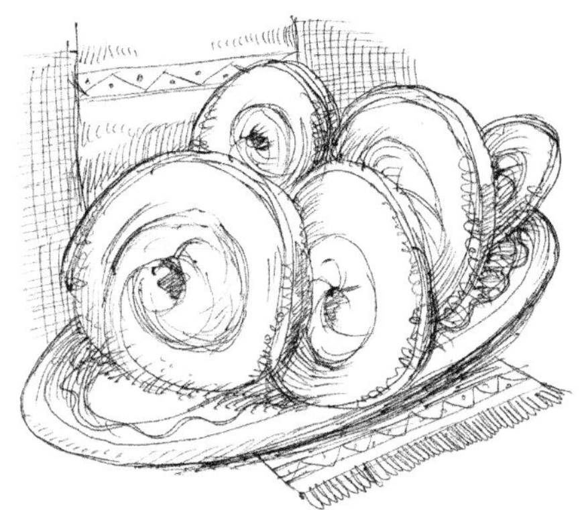

Sumy Shponder

1 kg pork belly
1 onion, peeled
1 parsley root, peeled and roughly chopped
1 small stalk celery, roughly chopped
2–3 cloves garlic
1–2 bay leaves
6–8 whole black peppercorns
5–6 allspice berries
½ teaspoon dried thyme
½ teaspoon dried basil
½ teaspoon dried coriander
½ teaspoon ground black pepper
3 teaspoons salt or to taste
3 tablespoons vinegar
1 teaspoon sugar or to taste

Place pork belly in a pot with about 5 cups of cold water. Bring to the boil, periodically skimming off the impurities that rise to the surface. Reduce the heat and add all the vegetables and spices, except for the garlic. Season with salt and pepper. Simmer on a very low heat for about 40–50 minutes.

Add vinegar, sugar and garlic about 5 minutes before the end of cooking. Let the pork belly cool in the stock it has been cooked in. Strain the stock (you can use the stock for another dish). Wrap the shponder in plastic wrap and refrigerate overnight. Serve chilled and sliced.

Saltseson

Saltseson, which is better known to English-speaking audience as head cheese, is considered a delicacy by many, but for the Ukrainian villagers who were accustomed to do their own butchering saltseson was one way to cook various cut-offs into a delicious dish.

500 g pork liver
2 pig's ears
1 pork heart
1 pork tongue
2 pork kidneys
300 g pork loin or shoulder
1 onion, peeled
1 carrot, peeled and roughly chopped
2 bay leaves
6–8 peppercorns
4–5 allspice berries
2 cloves garlic, crushed
Salt and ground black pepper to taste
1 pig's stomach (optional)
Kitchen string and needle (optional)

Separately cook pork liver in slightly salted water (see 'Simmered Liver' on page 99). Discard water.

Scrape and thoroughly wash the pig's ears under running cold water. Place into a pot with cold water and bring to the boil. Reduce the heat and simmer for about 5 minutes. Remove from the heat.

Trim off any membranes and as much fat as possible from the outside of the heart. Cut it in halves and remove the veins and arteries. Rinse under running cold water.

Thoroughly scrub the tongue, skin it, cut off the tubes and rinse in cold water.

Remove the fat and tubes from the kidneys and cut it into halves. Rinse thoroughly under running water.

Place ears, heart, tongue, kidneys, and loin or shoulder into a pot with cold water. The water should completely cover the ingredients. Bring to the boil, periodically skimming off the impurities that rise to the surface.

Add onion, carrot, bay leaves, peppercorns and allspice. Season with salt and pepper.

Simmer on a very low heat with a slightly open lid until the meats are cooked.

Each meat requires a different time to be cooked. When the meat is cooked, remove it from the pot and place in a bowl with a little of the stock to prevent it from drying. The ears will be cooked the longest, about 2–3 hours. They are done when a knife passes through them easily. Strain the stock and discard the vegetables and spices. Return all the meats (except for the liver) to the stock and bring back to the boil. Add garlic and remove from the heat.

Cut all the meats, including the liver, into small pieces. Add 1–1.5 cups of stock and mix.

If you are using a pig's stomach, clean, remove membrane, soak in salted warm water for about 3–4 hours and rinse it. Fill it with meat mixture about ¾ full. Sew the stomach edges securely. Place in a pot, cover it with hot salted water then bring to the boil. Reduce the heat and simmer for about 40 minutes. Place the saltseson into a large bowl. Let it cool slightly and place a light weight on top of it (for example, a chopping board and a plastic bottle with water on top). Let it set in the refrigerator overnight.

Alternatively, instead of a pig's stomach, use moulds covered with plastic wrap, which will make it easier to remove the saltseson when it sets. Place the cooked meat mixture into the moulds. Cover with a lid or plastic wrap. Leave in a refrigerator to set. To serve, remove the saltseson from the moulds.

Rye Poliadvytsia

1½ kg veal loin, boned
50 g smoked salo (or bacon for stuffing)
3 teaspoons salt or to taste
1 teaspoon ground black pepper
1 teaspoon ground allspice
½ teaspoon ground nutmeg
¼ cup rye flour for coating
Butter and oil for frying
½ cup sour cream

Slice the salo or bacon into thin strips and place in a freezer to harden. It will make it easier to insert them into the veal loin.

Make thin and deep incisions in the veal loin and insert the salo or bacon strips.

Rub the meat with salt, pepper, allspice and nutmeg. Coat in flour and fry in butter and oil in a frying pan on each side until golden brown. Move the veal loin into a roasting dish.

Add sour cream to the butter, oil and meat juices left in the frying pan and bring to the boil, stirring constantly. Pour the sour cream mixture over the meat.

Roast in a preheated oven at 180°C for 1–1.5 hours or until cooked to your liking. Serve hot or cold.

Cherry Silverside

1½ kg beef silverside
1 cup jarred morello cherries, pitted
3 teaspoons salt or to taste
1 teaspoon ground white pepper
½ teaspoon ground cloves
½ teaspoon ground cardamom
1 teaspoon ground cinnamon
3 tablespoons butter
½ cup morello cherry syrup
½ cup port wine

Make thin and deep incisions in the beef silverside and insert the cherries into the incisions. Thoroughly rub the meat with salt and spices.

Heat some butter in a frying pan and fry the beef on each side until golden brown to seal in the juices. Place the silverside on a roasting dish. Add cherry syrup and wine to the butter and meat juices left in the frying pan and bring to the boil, stirring constantly. Pour 3–4 tablespoons of the cherry syrup and wine mixture over the meat. Put the roasting tray in a preheated oven at 180°C for 1.5 hours or until cooked to your liking. Periodically keep drizzling with a few tablespoons of the cherry syrup and wine mixture over the meat. Serve hot or cold.

Velykden Leg of Lamb

1–1½ kg leg of lamb
4–5 cloves garlic
Salt and ground black pepper to taste
Oil and butter for frying
½ cup walnuts, roasted and chopped
½ cup raisins

Sauce:
1 cup stock (vegetable or chicken)
½ cup red wine
2 tablespoons brandy
1 tablespoon honey (optional)
4 rosemary sprigs
4–5 sage leaves

Trim off the excess fat from the lamb. With a thin, sharp knife make deep incisions over the surface of the lamb. Peel and halve or quarter the garlic cloves lengthways. Insert the garlic into the incisions. Rub the lamb thoroughly with salt and pepper.

Pan fry the lamb on each side in oil and butter until golden brown.

Keep the juices in the frying pan to make sauce. Place the lamb in a roasting pan and pour the sauce over it. Cover with a lid or foil and cook in preheated oven at 160°C for about 2.5 hours, periodically basting with the sauce.

Add walnuts and raisins to the sauce in the roasting pan. Cover with the foil and continue roasting for another 30–40 minutes.

Remove the foil and roast for 25–30 minutes or until lamb is golden brown. Remove from oven and leave to rest for about 15 minutes. Serve hot.

Sauce: Mix stock, wine, brandy and honey and add to the juices in the frying pan. Add rosemary and sage. Bring to the boil. Simmer for 1–2 minutes then remove from heat.

Mixed Pashtet

250 g veal
250 g pork (neck)
300 g cooked veal liver (see 'Simmered Liver' on page 99)
1 onion, peeled
1 carrot, peeled and roughly chopped
1 parsley root, peeled and roughly chopped
1 small stalk celery, roughly chopped
2–3 bay leaves
5–6 whole black peppercorns
6–8 allspice berries
2 eggs
Salt and ground black pepper to taste

Cooking meats: Place veal, pork and vegetables in a pot with about 1 litre (4 cups) of cold water. Bring to the boil, periodically skimming off the impurities that rise to the surface. Reduce the heat and add bay leaves, peppercorns and allspice. Season with salt and pepper to taste. Simmer for about 30–40 minutes, or until the meat is tender. If one of the meats cooks first, remove it, allowing the other meat to finish cooking. Remove the meat, carrot and parsley root. Strain the stock and return to the pot. Discard the rest of the vegetables and spices.

Making pashtet: Separate the egg yolks from egg whites and beat both. Combine veal, pork, veal liver and cooked vegetables then mince using a food processor. Add the egg yolks, 2–3 tablespoons of stock and season with salt and pepper to taste. Mince again. Carefully fold in the egg whites and place the mixture into the oiled oven-proof mould. Bake covered with a lid or aluminium foil in preheated oven at 170–180°C for about 40 minutes. Serve chilled.

Rich Pashtet

400 g liver (veal or beef)
1–2 cups milk (for soaking liver)
2 tablespoons plain flour
250 g button mushrooms, sliced
1 onion, peeled and sliced
Salt to taste
½ teaspoon ground allspice
½ teaspoon ground nutmeg
100 g butter, softened (plus butter for frying)

Clean the liver, removing membranes. Soak in milk for 1–2 hours. Cut the liver into slices.

Coat the liver slices in flour and fry in preheated butter on a very low heat on each side for about 5 minutes or until tender and no blood comes out when you pierce it. Let the liver cool to room temperature.

Sauté mushrooms and onion in butter for 4–5 minutes or until golden. Let them cool.

Mix the liver together with the sautéed vegetables and season with the salt and spices. Mince the mixture using a food processor. Add butter and mince again. Place the mixture in a mould and refrigerate. Serve chilled.

Salads

Salads are probably the least traditional dish among those that are served at Easter. The reason for that being that the holiday usually fell in early spring, before most common fresh salad vegetables like cucumbers and tomatoes had the chance to ripen – and stores of the previous year's harvest of potatoes, beetroots, carrots and other vegetables were running low. Nonetheless, with all the meat and other rich food being consumed at Easter, salads are a welcome addition to the table, and the Ukrainian cuisine offers a wonderful variety of salad dishes.

Vesna salad and tsvikli

Tsvikli

Also known as 'Buriachky', 'Tsvikli' can be served as a salad or relish.

2 beetroots
4–5 tablespoons finely grated horseradish
¼ cup beetroot kvas (see 'Pickled Beetroot and Kvas' on page 101) (optional)
1–2 tablespoons vinegar (optional, or lemon juice)
Salt and sugar to taste

Cook beetroots whole with the skin on. Let them cool. Finely grate the beetroots and mix with horseradish. Alternatively, combine with the beetroot kvas or vinegar. Season with salt and sugar to taste then stir well.

Beetroot and Prunes Salad

2–3 beetroots
1 cup prunes
½ cup walnuts, roasted and chopped
2 cloves garlic, peeled and crushed
Salt to taste

Dressing:
2 tablespoons mayonnaise (see 'Home-made Mayonnaise' on page 79 or use sour cream, melted butter, oil)

Cook beetroots whole with the skin on. Let them cool, then peel and coarsely grate. Thinly slice the prunes (alternatively, if the prunes are hard, soak them in warm water for 15–30 minutes, or until soft). Mix together beetroot, prunes, walnuts, garlic and dressing. Season with salt to taste and stir well.

Vesna Salad

5–6 eggs, hard-boiled and peeled
6–8 red radishes
5 spring onions, chopped
½ teaspoon salt or to taste
¼ cup sour cream (full-cream)

Slice the eggs into 8 pieces each. Thinly slice radishes. Lightly toss eggs, radishes and onions and season with salt. Pour the sour cream on the bottom of a serving dish and toss the vegetables on top.

Mizeria Salad

3–4 cucumbers
1 teaspoon salt
1 tablespoon vinegar
¼ cup spring onion, finely chopped
½ tablespoon dill or parsley, finely chopped (optional)
2 tablespoons oil (or ¼ cup sour cream)

Peel the cucumbers and slice thinly. Sprinkle with salt and set aside in a sieve for about 10 minutes. Press out excess juice. Add vinegar, onion and dill or parsley then toss. Dress with oil or sour cream.

Mixed Radish Salad

1 white radish
5–6 red radishes
1–2 cucumbers (optional)
½ tablespoon dill, chopped
½ teaspoon salt or to taste
¼ cup sour cream

Peel and coarsely grate white radish. Sprinkle with salt and set aside in a sieve for about 10 minutes. Press out excess juice. Thinly slice red radishes. Optionally, slice cucumbers. Mix all the ingredients and serve.

Cabbage with Prunes and Carrot

½ cabbage
6–8 prunes
1 carrot
½ teaspoon salt or to taste

Dressing:
1 tablespoon lemon juice or apple cider vinegar
1 tablespoon honey
2 tablespoons oil

Finely julienne the cabbage. Season with salt and squeeze to soften it a little and let some of its juice out.

Thinly slice the prunes. Alternatively, if the prunes are hard, soak them in warm water for 15–30 minutes, or until soft, then strain and slice.

Peel and coarsely grate the carrot.

Toss the vegetables together.

Mix lemon juice, or vinegar, with honey and oil to make the dressing. Pour the dressing over the vegetables and toss again.

Cabbage and Kovbasa Salad

½ cabbage
300 g smoked kovbasa or ham
1 cucumber
3 red radishes
½ teaspoon salt or to taste

Dressing:
2 hard-boiled egg yolks
3 tablespoons sour cream
1 tablespoon dill or parsley, chopped
1 clove garlic, peeled and crushed
Salt and ground black pepper to taste.

Finely julienne the cabbage. Season with salt and squeeze to soften it a little and let out some of its juice.

Thinly julienne kovbasa or ham, cucumber and radishes.

Toss everything together. Drizzle salad dressing on top and serve.

Making dressing: Crush egg yolks with a fork. Add sour cream one tablespoon at a time, mixing constantly. Season with salt and pepper. Add dill or parsley and garlic then mix everything together.

U Seli Salad

3 potatoes, boiled in jacket
4 hard-boiled eggs
300–400 g cooked meat (roasted or boiled pork, veal or lamb)
2–3 pickled gherkins

Dressing:
½ cup sour cream
1 tablespoon mustard
Salt and ground black or white pepper to taste

Peel the potatoes and eggs. Slice meat and potatoes into small cubes. Finely chop the eggs and gherkins. Mix everything together. Add dressing and mix again.

Making dressing: In a small bowl combine sour cream and mustard. Season with salt and pepper and lightly whisk with a fork.

Relishes, Sauces and Dressings

With the various meat dishes cooked for Easter celebrations, it is only appropriate to have a few relishes and sauces on the table to highlight their flavour. Horseradish, being a traditional item to be included in the Easter basket, is one of the most popular main ingredients for relishes and sauces cooked for this occasion. Horseradish is closely followed by mustard. *Kholodets* (see 'Kholodets' on page 56), for example, is barely ever served without the accompaniment of one of these two relishes.

Mayonnaise, although not a long-standing traditional dish in Ukraine became a very popular salad dressing over the last century. A recipe for home-made mayonnaise is also offered in this chapter.

Berry sauce, mint honey sauce, home-made mayonnaise, rum mustard and horseradish sauce

Punchy Horseradish Sauce

2 raw egg yolks
½ cup sour cream
1 cup horseradish, finely grated
Salt and ground black pepper to taste

In a small saucepan, mix the egg yolks with sour cream until the mixture is smooth. Add horseradish and season with salt and pepper. Stirring constantly, bring the mixture to the boil then remove from heat.

Horseradish Sauce

1 cup horseradish, finely grated
2 tablespoons butter
¼ cup sour cream or cream
1 tablespoon lemon
Salt and sugar to taste

If your horseradish is freshly grated it can, optionally, be scalded and then strained. Fry horseradish in preheated butter for 1–2 minutes. Add sour cream or cream and, stirring constantly, bring to the boil. Season with salt and sugar to taste. Remove from the heat and add lemon juice. Stir thoroughly.

Horseradish and Herb Relish

½ cup horseradish, finely grated
1 cup sour cream
3–4 eggs, hard-boiled
1 tablespoon parsley, finely chopped
1 tablespoon dill, finely chopped
2 tablespoons spring onions, finely chopped
Salt and sugar to taste

Mash egg yolks with a fork. Add 2 tablespoons of sour cream and mix until smooth. Finely chop egg whites. Mix all the ingredients and season with salt and sugar.

Horseradish and Apple Relish

½ cup horseradish, finely grated
1 tablespoon boiling water
2 apples, peeled and finely grated
2–3 tablespoons cream
Salt and sugar to taste

Mix horseradish with water, salt and sugar. Let the mixture cool. Add apples and cream then mix again.

Mint Honey Sauce

½ cup honey
1/3 cup lemon juice (or 2 tablespoons apple cider vinegar)
½ cup vegetable stock
1 teaspoon dried mint
2 tablespoons butter
Salt to taste

In a small saucepan, combine all the ingredients. Bring to the boil. Reduce the heat and simmer for 3–4 minutes. Remove from the heat. Optionally, strain the sauce. Serve hot or cold.

Rum Mustard

2 tablespoons mustard seeds
½ cup mustard powder
1 teaspoon salt
1 teaspoon turmeric
¼ cup white wine vinegar
3 tablespoons honey
2 tablespoons rum
1 tablespoon oil

Crush mustard seeds using a mortar and pestle or using a food processor. Mix them with mustard powder, salt and turmeric. Gradually add vinegar, stirring constantly. Add honey, rum and oil. Mix everything thoroughly. You will notice that the mixture will start to thicken.

Let the mustard stand at room temperature for about 10–15 minutes. Place the mustard in jars. For the first 2 weeks cover the jars with two layers of greaseproof paper. Afterwards use normal lids.

Store the mustard in a refrigerator. The mustard is ready in 2–3 days; however, it tastes even better in 8–10 days.

Home-made Mayonnaise

2 egg yolks
1 tablespoon lemon juice
1 tablespoon vinegar
½ teaspoon mustard powder
½ teaspoon salt or to taste
½ teaspoon sugar
1 cup oil (sunflower or canola)

Combine egg yolks, lemon juice and vinegar. In a separate small bowl combine the dry ingredients, and then add to the egg mixture. Whisk until blended.

Gradually and in very small quantities, about a couple of drops at a time, add half a cup of oil, whisking constantly until the mixture thickens. Continually whisking add the remaining half a cup of oil, one tablespoon at a time. Keep refrigerated.

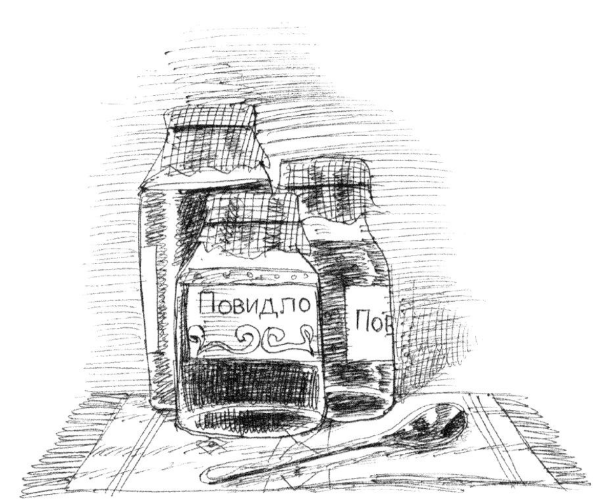

Berry Sauce

1 cup berry jam (choice of cranberry, black currant or red currant)
¼ cup water
½ tablespoon butter
1 tablespoon lemon juice
¼ teaspoon ground cloves
¼ teaspoon ground nutmeg
Salt and ground white pepper to taste

Combine all the ingredients in a small saucepan. Bring to the boil, stirring constantly, then remove from heat. Let it cool to room temperature

Savoury Baked Goods and Desserts

One would think that having all the flavoursome *pasky* that are customarily baked for Easter celebrations (see 'Paska – the Specialty Bread for Ukrainian Easter' on page 13) might render other baked goods unnecessary, but when it comes to Ukrainian Velykden there can never be enough mouth-watering and fragrant breads and desserts. There is always room on the Easter table for some more sweet and savoury *pyrizhky*, rohalyky, verhuny and a cake or two.

Ukrainian traditional desserts, including medivnyk (honey cake), makivnyk (poppy-seed roll), rohalyky (rolled-up biscuits in the form of horns with a filling inside), verhuny (deep-fried thin biscuits) and others are common dishes on the Ukrainian Easter table. All of these desserts have been a part of the Ukrainian cuisine for a very long time. They might not be as fashionable now as some time ago, but thanks to their delicious qualities they firmly keep their position on the Ukrainian table. This chapter also offers a couple of recipes for torte, a layered cake with filling, which in Ukraine is called 'tort' or 'pliatsok'.

The recipes below are just a few favourites that are baked on the occasion of Easter throughout many regions of Ukraine.

Walnut torte, makivnyk and domashni rohalyky

Three Accounts of Velykden Feast Preparations

As ancient as a nation's traditions are, they remain fragile and potentially affected by major developments such as colonisation, a new ruling regime, or sweeping social, economic and technological changes. At any point in history it could take just one generation failing to teach the next about special rituals or retelling a piece of lore that has not been recorded, and these folk treasures will be lost forever. The people of Ukraine, fortunately, have consistently held a strong drive to preserve the nation's identity through cultural traditions. Despite centuries of prohibitions, suppression of the language, literature and culture, the Holodomor, forced resettlement, exiles and death penalties, the people of Ukraine found enough strength to preserve many ancient customs, rituals and beliefs.

The assistance of Ukrainian amateur and professional ethnographers – people dedicated to recording the nation's lore, customs, and daily life – also played an enormous part in this preservation.

There is barely a single Ukrainian ethnographer who, when recording the traditions and rituals of the Ukrainian people, omitted to write about the Velykden (Easter) celebrations. Following are excerpts relevant to the Easter meal and its preparations. The extracts feature three well-known Ukrainian ethnographers, Mykola Markevych, Volodymyr Shukhevych and Fedir Vovk.

A most poetic account of Easter celebrations is found in the monograph of 19th century ethnographer Mykola Markevych: *Ukrainians' Customs, Folk Beliefs, Foods and Beverages.* In this excerpt the famous Ukrainian ethnographer describes an 1850 Easter feast at the home of a well-to-do Pan (lord):

> At last Easter arrived! This is the time when Ukrainian hospitality is mostly evident: around the church there are carts with food brought to be blessed [...]. There is no man who would not have on the day a piglet, *kovbasa*, *paska* and several *krashanky*. Here is a description of a wealthy Pan, whose Pani [lord's wife] follows the native traditions: two, three or even four huge sweet *pasky* made from outstanding best quality wheat flour, butter, eggs and sugar; one or two savoury *pasky*; cheese paska, a couple of piglets – one without stuffing and one stuffed with kasha and liver; they both have horseradish in the mouth, two lambs – one without stuffing and one stuffed with almonds, raisins and rice; ham and *buzhenyna*; a whole head of boar, with olives instead of eyes stuck in butter; spring onions; green salad; pieces of outstanding *salo*; several types of *kovbasa* – *krovyanka* [black pudding], traditional, liver *kovbasa* and others; butter, cheese, sour cream and onion; all that is surrounded by eggs dyed in blue, yellow, marble and mostly red; these are duck and chicken eggs. Added to this are several kinds of *horilka* and *nalyvka.*

Volodymyr Shukhevych wrote a multi-volume work on Hutsul life in the 19th century which is a real well of knowledge for the Hutsul traditions and rituals. Shukhevych's observations offer some insights into the typical Easter preparations of a Hutsul family in an ordinary village.

> On Holy Saturday they finish their farming chores; and in the afternoon the mistress of the house starts preparing the meal. She slices beetroots and sets the *borshch* to be cooked, having added salted and smoked meats to it; and after that she cooks eggs. [...]
>
> When the first *paska*, which is intended to be blessed at the church, is baked, they put it in the middle of the table and then they bake smaller *pasky* [...] and other goods; in some villages they also bake "stilnyk-zastivnyk", a large loaf of bread, in which they stick, with the rounded end down, as many eggs for as many souls in the family; if one of the eggs cracks while baking, it foretells the death of the one for whom the egg was intended. "Stilnyk" is placed next to the first *paska* on the table.

In 1928, the Ukrainian community in Prague published *Studies on Ukrainian Ethnography and Anthropology*. This extensive work was written by professor Fedir Vovk. In this volume the professor presented an array of folk customs related to various special occasions, including folk and religious feasts such as Easter:

> On Easter, according to a widespread belief, the sun is "playing", that is, at dawn it keeps rising and then descending over the horizon; and there are many people, especially children, who try not to oversleep this moment. After *rozhovyny* every farmer tries to climb the bell tower and ring the bell to ensure a good harvest of buckwheat. In Ukraine the ritual dishes for Easter consist of: *pasky*, which are round wheat loafs of bread; roasted piglet; *kovbasa*; cheese; and especially *krashanky*, which are eggs that are dyed in all sorts of colours, especially red. These eggs have no direct Christian meaning, but are associated with certain legends. When exchanging good wishes, people give each other *krashanky*, but even more often *pysanky* [...]

Despite fewer surviving traditions and customs being practised now, you will still know that it is Velykden in Ukraine without consulting the calendar and you can experience the joy of this beautiful ancient holiday on the streets of any Ukrainian village or city.

Boryshnyk

5–6 potatoes, boiled in jacket
1 egg, lightly beaten
3 tablespoons flour
3 tablespoons cornmeal
Salt to taste
Oil for frying

Making boryshnyk dough: Peel and mash the potatoes. Combine with egg, flour and cornmeal and season with salt. Knead the dough well until it stops sticking to the hand. The dough should be soft. You can bake or pan-fry the boryshnyk.

Baking boryshnyk: Roll out dough and place into an oiled 2–3 cm deep baking dish. Bake in a preheated oven at 180°C for 20–25 minutes or until golden.

Pan-frying boryshnyk: Roll out dough slightly smaller then the size of a frying pan. Place in preheated and oiled frying pan and fry on each side for 5–6 minutes or until golden brown.

Serve hot or cold. Also, you can reheat boryshnyk in a frying pan. In this case, slice boryshnyk into serving pieces and fry in butter on both sides until golden. This Hutsul dish usually accompanies *kholodets* (see 'Kholodets' on page 56) and generally can be used instead of bread.

Potato and Ham Babka

3 potatoes, boiled in jacket
250 g ham
4 eggs
¼ cup cream (or sour cream)
1–2 cloves garlic, peeled and crushed
½ teaspoon dried thyme
Salt and ground black pepper to taste

Peel and coarsely grate the potatoes. Chop the ham finely. Gently mix potato and ham together.

Separate the egg yolks and whites into two separate bowls. Combine egg yolks, cream or sour cream, garlic and thyme. Season the mixture with salt and pepper and whisk until smooth. Separately beat the egg whites until they are stiff.

Add the egg yolk mixture to the potato and ham then mix. Fold in egg whites carefully. Place the mixture into a greased baking pan and bake in a preheated oven at 180°C for 25–30 minutes or until cooked through.

Velykden Pyrizhky

Dough:
450–500 g plain flour
14 g yeast
1 cup milk
2 teaspoons sugar, plus ¼ cup sugar for sweet pyrizhky
80 g butter, melted and lukewarm
1 egg, plus 1 egg for brushing
2 egg yolks
2 tablespoons sour cream
½ teaspoon salt

Filling:
Choose filling from 'Pyrizhky Fillings'

Making dough: Dissolve yeast in lukewarm milk with a pinch of sugar and 1 tablespoon of flour. Set aside to rise for 10–15 minutes.

Lightly beat the egg and egg yolks. Mix the butter, egg mixture, sour cream, sugar and salt. Combine with the yeast mixture. Sift the flour in a bowl, make a well in the centre and pour in the mixture.

Knead until the dough becomes smooth. Place the dough in a bowl, cover it with plastic wrap and let it rise for about 1 hour. The dough should double in size. Knead the dough again and leave it to rise for the second time for 30–40 minutes.

Forming pyrizhky: Divide the dough into manageable portions (3 or 4). Take one portion, keeping the rest under plastic wrap, to prevent the dough drying out. Cut off small, approximately egg-sized, pieces of dough. Roll or flatten each piece into a round base about 5 mm thick and put filling in the centre. Bring the edges together and pinch together firmly. The centre of the pyrizhky should be plump, keeping 'a spur' from the pinched edges in the centre of the pyrizhok. You can choose to have 'a spur' on the bottom or top of the pyrizhok. Repeat with the rest of the bases.

Forming pyrizhky with 'Sweet Cheese Filling': A very popular shape for sweet cheese pyrizhky is formed as follows. After flattening the round bases, make two incisions, about 2 cm long, on the opposite sides of the bases, about 1 cm from its edges. Place the filling in the middle and flip the sides with incisions over the filling, stretching them a little. The stretched incisions create an opening for the filling.

Baking pyrizhky: Place pyrizhky 2.5–3 cm apart on a baking tray covered with baking paper and let them rise for 30–40 minutes in a warm place. Brush the pyrizhky with a lightly beaten egg. Bake in a preheated oven at 180°C for 20–25 minutes or until golden.

Makivnyk

Poppy seed filling:
2 cups poppy seeds
2 tablespoons honey
2 tablespoons butter
¾ cup sugar
⅓ cup walnuts, roasted and chopped
¼ cup raisins
¼ cup candied orange zest
3 egg whites

Dough:
350–400 g flour, plus extra for dusting
14 g yeast
½ cup milk, lukewarm
½ cup sugar
3 egg yolks, plus 1 egg yolk for brushing
¼ cup butter, melted and cooled down
¼ teaspoon salt
¼ teaspoon vanilla extract

Poppy seed filling: Cover the poppy seeds with boiling water and let them sit for 15–20 minutes. Strain the water. Crush the poppy seeds using a mortar and pestle or using a food processor.

Place honey and butter in a small saucepan and bring to the boil. Remove from the heat and add other ingredients except for the egg whites. Mix well and let the mixture cool until lukewarm.

Just before rolling the filling into the dough beat the egg whites until stiff then gently fold into the poppy seed mixture.

Making dough: Dissolve the yeast and 1 tablespoon of sugar in milk. Leave in a warm place to rise for 15 minutes.

Add sugar to the egg yolks and whisk until the mixture is smooth and pale yellow.

Combine yeast mixture, butter, egg yolk mixture, salt and vanilla. Gradually add into the sifted flour. Knead until the dough becomes smooth. Leave it in a warm place for about 1 hour to rise. The dough should double in size. Knead the dough again and leave it to rise for another 30–40 minutes.

Forming and baking rolls: Knead the dough again, divide into 2 parts and roll out into rectangle bases on a floured surface. The bases should be about 3–5 mm thick.

Spread the filling, leaving about 2 cm edges on all sides. Roll the bases from the long side. Do not press too hard to avoid squashing the filling. Optionally, tuck the edges inside to prevent filling from escaping.

Place the rolls on a baking tray covered with baking paper. Cover with a tea towel and let them rise for 20–25 minutes in a warm place. Brush the rolls with the egg yolk. Bake in a preheated oven at 180°C for 30–35 minutes, or until they turn a golden-brown colour.

Konotop Verhuny

2 cups flour
3 eggs
2 tablespoons milk
Zest from 1 lemon
1 tablespoon lemon juice
¼ cup sugar
¼ teaspoon salt
Oil for deep frying
Caster or icing sugar for dusting

Lightly whisk eggs and milk. Gradually add lemon zest and juice, sugar and salt. Gradually add into the sifted flour. Knead until the dough becomes smooth. Leave it for 15 minutes to rest covered in plastic wrap.

Roll out the dough into 2–3 mm thick bases. Cut into strips, for example, 3 cm × 10 cm in size. The strips should be small enough to fit into a pan for deep frying. Make small cuts in the middle of both ends of each strip and in the centre. Take one end of the strip and carefully pull it through the cut in the centre. Repeat this process with each strip.

Heat oil in a deep pan. Deep-fry verhuny for about 1 minute on each side or until golden brown. Using a slotted spoon, transfer to a paper towel to absorb excess oil. Let them cool. Dust with caster or icing sugar.

Domashni Rohalyky

Dough:
2¾ cup flour (plus extra for dusting)
1 teaspoon baking soda
1 teaspoon vinegar
200 g butter, melted and lukewarm
½ cup sour cream
A pinch of salt
1 egg for brushing

Cherry Filling:
1 cup morello cherries, pitted and strained (jarred or fresh)

Berry Filling:
Thick berry jam

Walnut Filling:
1 cup walnuts, roasted and ground
1 egg white
½ cup sugar
A few drops of vanilla extract

Making dough: Sift the flour in a bowl and make a well in the centre. Place baking soda into a larger spoon and pour vinegar on top. The baking soda will froth. Pour it into the flour well. Add the butter, sour cream and salt. Knead the dough. Cover in plastic wrap and refrigerate for 15–20 minutes.

Forming rohalyky: Divide dough into 2–3 manageable parts. Take one part and roll out into a thin round base. Cut the base into 12 equal slices (pizza-like segments). Place the filling of your choice near the edge of each slice. Roll the slice with your hand towards the centre. Do not press too hard to avoid squashing the filling. Alternatively, tuck the edges inside to prevent filling from escaping.

Place the rohalyky on a baking tray, brush with a lightly beaten egg. Bake in an oven at 170°C for about 25 minutes or until golden.

Making walnut filling: Beat the egg white until stiff. Gradually add the sugar and vanilla, beating continually. Gently add the egg-white mixture to the walnuts, stirring constantly.

Syrnyk

600 g cheese
¼ cup raisins
4 eggs
½ cup sugar
2 tablespoons semolina
2 tablespoons butter, softened
A few drops of vanilla extract
1 tablespoon of flour (for coating raisins)
Oil for baking
1–2 tablespoons breadcrumbs for dusting

Rub the cheese through a sieve, or cream it using a blender or food processor.

In a small bowl cover the raisins with boiling water for about 10 minutes then strain.

Separate the egg whites from the yolks into two bowls. Add the sugar to the egg yolks and whisk until the mixture is smooth and pale yellow. Add semolina, butter and vanilla then mix thoroughly.

Combine the egg yolk mixture and cheese then beat until light and fluffy. Toss the raisins in flour and stir into the mixture.

Separately beat the egg whites until they are stiff and carefully fold into the cheese mixture.

Place the mixture into a baking dish that has been oiled and dusted with breadcrumbs. Bake syrnyk in a water bath or bain-marie (place the baking dish into a larger pan containing water) in a preheated oven at 180°C for 1 hour or until cooked through.

Medivnyk Torte

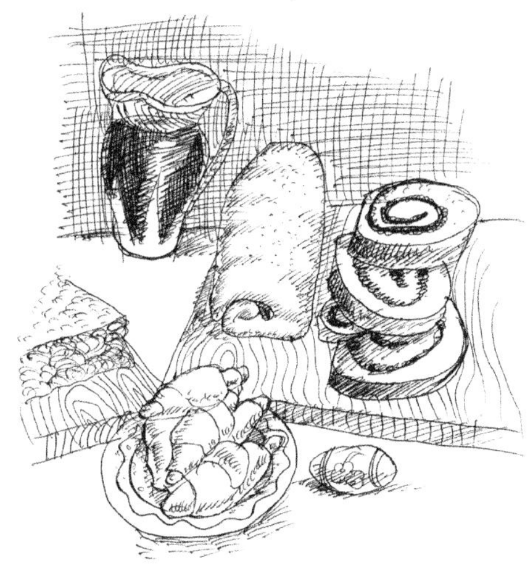

Batter:
3 cups flour
2 cups sugar
1½ teaspoons baking soda
1 tablespoon vinegar
60 g butter
2–3 tablespoons honey
5 eggs

Filling:
600 g light sour cream
1 cup sugar

Making batter: Mix the flour and sugar. Place soda on a tablespoon and cover with vinegar. The ingredients will start fizzing. Stir the soda with a teaspoon, ensuring that as much of it as possible reacts with vinegar. Add to the flour mixture. Melt the butter, let it cool and mix with the honey. Lightly beat the eggs. Mix everything together until smooth. Place the mixture into the top of a double boiler and stir it constantly over simmering water for about 10–15 minutes. The texture and the colour of the mixture will change.

Spoon some of the batter on the greased baking tray and, using the back of the spoon or a knife, gently spread the batter thinly and evenly. Using tray size 22 × 28 cm you will get 4 layers. Bake in a preheated oven at 180–190°C for 7–10 minutes or until golden brown. Let the layers cool down. Join them together with the filling and spread it over the top.

Making filling: Whip the sour cream with sugar until light and smooth and almost doubled in volume.

Walnut Torte

Batter:
10 eggs
200 g sugar
200 g walnuts, roasted and ground
½ cup flour
Zest of 1 lemon, grated (optional)

Filling:
100 g walnuts, roasted and ground
100 g almonds, roasted and ground
100 g icing sugar
5 egg yolks

Icing:
100 g walnuts, roasted and ground
½ cup milk
100 g sugar
120 g butter, softened
1 tablespoon lemon juice

Making batter: Separate the egg whites from the yolks into 2 bowls. Add the sugar to the egg yolks and whisk until the mixture is smooth and pale yellow. Mix walnuts, flour and lemon zest. Gradually add the egg yolk mixture to the walnut mixture, stirring it in gently. Separately beat the egg whites until they are stiff then fold them into the walnut mixture. Divide the batter into two equal portions. Spread each portion on the greased baking trays and bake in a preheated oven at 180°C for 8–10 minutes or until golden brown. Let the layers cool down. Join them together with the filling. Spread the icing on top.

Making filling: Mix all the ingredients in a small saucepan. Stirring constantly, simmer on a very low heat for about 2 minutes or until the mixture thickens. Remove from the heat and let it cool.

Making icing: Add walnuts to the milk in a small saucepan. Stirring constantly, simmer on a low heat for about 2–3 minutes. Remove from heat and let cool. Beat butter with sugar until fluffy. Combine both mixtures and add lemon juice. Mix well.

Pyrizhky Fillings

Cheese and Dill Filling

2 cups cheese (syr, quark or bryndza)
1 egg
1 tablespoon dill
Salt and ground black pepper to taste

Rub the cheese through a sieve and mix with lightly whisked egg. Season with salt and pepper then stir in chopped dill.

Sweet Cheese Filling

2 cups cheese (syr, quark or bryndza)
2 egg yolks
¼ cup raisins
¼ cup sugar or to taste
¼ teaspoon salt

Rub the cheese through a sieve, or cream it using a blender or food processor.

In a small bowl cover the raisins with boiling water for about 10 minutes, then strain.

Add egg yolks, raisins, sugar and salt to the cheese and mix thoroughly.

Poppy Seed Filling

1½–2 cups poppy seeds
½ cup sugar or to taste

Cover the poppy seeds with boiling water and let them sit for 15–20 minutes. Strain the water. Crush the poppy seeds using a mortar and pestle (or in a food processor). Mix the crushed poppy seeds with sugar and continue crushing for another 5 minutes.

Rice Filling

2 cups cooked rice
2 tablespoons butter, softened
4 eggs, hard-boiled and chopped
¼ cup chopped spring onion
Salt and ground black pepper to taste

Mix cooked rice with butter. Combine rice, eggs and spring onion then season with salt and pepper.

Liver and Potato Filling

300 g cooked liver (beef, pork or poultry) (see 'Simmered Liver' on page 99)
2–3 potatoes
1 onion
Butter for frying
Salt to taste

Peel and cut potatoes into cubes. Boil in slightly salted water. When potatoes are cooked, discard the water.

Peel and finely chop the onion. Sauté in butter until golden brown.

Mix liver, potato and onion together. Season with salt and mince the mixture using a food processor.

Home-Made Pantry Staples

Some of the Ukrainian traditional dishes are rather complex and are based on two or more components, which are cooked separately and often using different cooking techniques. These components are then combined together at the final stages of the cooking process, thus creating one dish. A good example is 'Velykden Borshch' (see 'Borshch and Soup' on page 29). The recipe is based on fermented beetroot *kvas*, simmered ham stock, roasted beetroots and sautéed carrot and onion.

Such components as beetroot *kvas* and ham stock are also used in other recipes offered in this book. They have been gathered together in a separate chapter as they require both time to prepare and some additional ingredients. Also, as they are the components of many recipes it means cooking them in larger quantities can be a great time-saver.

Home-made pantry staples: ham stock and pickled beetroot and kvas

Simmered Liver

600–700 g liver (or according to your chosen recipe)
½ litre milk (for soaking liver)
1 onion, peeled
1–2 bay leaves
3–4 black peppercorns
4–6 allspice berries
Salt to taste

Cooking beef or pork liver: Clean the liver, removing membranes. Soak in milk for at least 30 minutes and preferably for about 2 hours.

Put liver, onion, bay leaves, peppercorns and allspice into a pot with boiling water. Season with salt to taste. Bring back to the boil then reduce the heat and simmer for 10–15 minutes, or until the liver is tender. Do not overcook the liver, otherwise it will go tough and rubbery. To check whether the liver is cooked, pierce it with a skewer: no sign of blood from the incision means it is time to stop cooking. Discard the onion and spices.

Cooking poultry liver: Clean the liver, removing membranes. There is no need to soak the poultry liver in milk. Cook the same way as beef or pork liver but for a shorter period of time, approximately 6–8 minutes. Pierce to check for readiness.

Simmered Tongue

1–2 beef (or veal) tongues
2 carrots, peeled and quartered
1 onion, peeled
2–3 bay leaves
4–6 whole black peppercorns
Salt to taste

Thoroughly scrub the tongues and rinse in cold water. Place tongues and the rest of the ingredients in a pot and cover with boiling water. Bring back to the boil, reduce the heat and simmer for 3–4 hours or until tender (it takes less time to cook veal tongue, about 2–2.5 hours). Place the tongues into the iced cold water to help loosen the skin. Peel off the outer skin and cut off the tubes.

Ham Stock

After shaving off the best-looking slices from the ham on the bone to serve as a part of the Easter plate of delectable cold meats, a bone with some leftover pieces of meat on it remains. This not-so-pretty product makes one of the most flavoursome and full-bodied stocks. In fact, the rest of the ingredients listed in this recipe are just extras to offer some variation on the traditional flavour. A few can be selected or they can be omitted entirely.

700–800 g ham on the bone
1 onion, peeled
1–2 carrots, peeled and quartered
1 parsley root, peeled and quartered
3–4 stalks celery, quartered
1 bay leaf
1 teaspoon dried thyme
1 teaspoon dried parsley
3–4 cloves
6–8 black peppercorns
3 cloves garlic, crushed

Place ham in a pot and cover with 2.5–3 litres cold water. Bring to the boil and add the rest of the ingredients, except for the garlic. Simmer on a low heat for 2–3 hours.

Add garlic 3–5 minutes before the end of cooking. Strain stock and, optionally, skim off fat.

Trim the meat from the bone and return to the stock or reserve for other recipes. Discard the bone, the skin (if any), and the vegetables and spices.

Pickled Beetroot and Kvas

4–5 beetroots
1–1½ litres lukewarm water

Place whole unpeeled beetroots in a saucepan and cover with water. Bring to the boil, decrease the heat and when the beetroots are almost cooked – about 25 minutes depending on the size of the vegetables – remove them from the saucepan. Allow the beetroots to cool then peel them.

You can either quarter or julienne the beetroots. The julienned beetroots will ferment faster and the kvas will be ready sooner.

In addition to the liquid, that is the 'kvas', the beetroot itself can be used in cooking, for example, in borshch (see 'Velykden Borshch' on page 32). Julienned beetroot is added to the dish as is, whereas the quartered beetroot needs to be julienned first and then added to the recipe.

Place the quartered or julienned beetroots in a glass jar. Optionally, place a dry slice of rye bread on top of the beetroot. You can wrap the bread slice in cheesecloth to prevent the bread from falling apart when it absorbs the water. The rye bread will speed up the fermentation process. Pour the lukewarm water over the beetroots, completely covering them. Cover the jar with a piece of open-weave cloth and leave it in a warm place to ferment for about 3–5 days.

When the kvas has finished fermenting, you may use it or seal the jar and store it in a refrigerator.

Optionally, if you are not using the beetroots as an ingredient in another dish, you can use them to make a second batch of kvas. To do that, strain the kvas into a different jar or bottle, replace the slice of bread and cover the beetroots with water again. When the second batch of kvas is ready, strain it then discard the bread and beetroots.

Glossary

Baba – See *babka* definition.

Babka (*babky*, plural; also *baba*) – (1) The synonym of *paska* (see definition); (2) A baked or steamed pudding. Many of the recipes require beaten egg whites, which ensure the *babka* will rise. *Babka* ingredients may also include: vegetables, fruit, cooked pasta, rice and so on.

Borshch (*borshchi*, plural) – Also commonly spelt *borsch or borscht*, this is a traditional Ukrainian soup, the main ingredient of which is beetroot. Another variation is *zelenyi* (green) *borshch* made from sorrel or other herbs and leaf vegetables. Other ingredients may include: cabbage, potatoes, tomatoes, carrots, onions, garlic, dill, meat, fish and so on.

Bryndza – This sheep milk cheese is somewhat similar in taste to feta cheese. It is one of the most popular cheeses in the Carpathian area of Ukraine.

Buzhenyna (also *shynka*) – Either smoked or roasted, this is a large piece of meat, most often pork, (usually no less than 1 kg). Prior to smoking or roasting, the piece of meat is marinated or precooked (boiled) or stuffed with spices, onions, garlic, salo and so on.

Driapanka (*driapanky*, plural) – Along with *krashanka*, *pysanka* and *krapanka*, this is a Ukrainian traditional Easter egg. The name *driapanka* is derived from the verb 'driapaty' (Engl., 'to scratch'). As the name suggests, the decoration on the egg (usually the surface is dyed in a dark colour beforehand) is created by scratching with a sharp object.

Horilka – This Ukrainian distilled spirit has an average 40% alcoholic content. The Russian equivalent of *horilka* is vodka. The name *horilka* is derived from 'hority' (Engl., 'to burn').

Kholodets – This is a jellied (aspic) fish, meat and fruit dish. Other popular names for the dish are 'studenets', 'zalyvne' and 'drahli'.

Kovbasa (*kovbasy*, plural) – The name can refer to various kinds of smoked, boiled or fried meat sausages.

Krapanka (*krapanky*, plural) – Along with *driapanka* the *krapanka* is a lesser-known Ukrainian traditional Easter egg. It is not as sophisticated in its design as *pysanka*, because its only symbol is a dot. Its name, *krapanka*, is derived from 'krapaty' (Engl., 'to drip') or 'krapka' (Engl., 'drop').

Krashanka (*krashanky*, plural) – Along with the *pysanka*, the *krashanka* is the most popular of the Ukrainian traditional Easter eggs. *Krashanky* are usually one-colour dyed eggs and they are edible: the raw eggs are boiled in a dyeing solution (see 'The Magical Dyed Egg – Krashanka' on page 36).

Kvas – Usually, *kvas* refers to a traditional sweet-and-sour fermented beverage. Beetroot *kvas* is rarely used for drinking. This fermented product was once an essential ingredient of *borshch* and other dishes, adding a pleasing sourness to the taste. In the early 1900's the beetroot *kvas* was largely replaced with tomato products.

Nalyvka – This sweet fruit or berry alcoholic beverage is produced by fermenting fruit or berries in sugar. Often *horilka* is added to fortify the drink.

Paska (*pasky*, plural; also *baba* and *babka*) – This is a ritual Ukrainian Easter bread (see 'Paska – the Specialty Bread for Ukrainian Easter' on page 13).

Pokuttia – The special corner of an old-fashioned Ukrainian house, where the icons are placed, is called the *pokuttia*. The corner was considered to be an honourable place.

Pyrih (*pyrohy*, plural) – This sweet or savoury pie is usually made from yeast-raised dough (sometimes shortcrust or puff pastry) and has various fillings, including: mashed potatoes, minced cooked meat, fish, eggs, cheese, fruits, berries and so on.

Pyrizhky (*pyrizhok*, singular) – These baked, pan-fried or deep-fried sweet or savoury buns can have meat, cheese or vegetarian fillings.

Pysanka (*pysanky*, plural) – Along with the *krashanka*, the *pysanka* is the most popular of the Ukrainian traditional Easter eggs. *Pysanky* are exquisitely decorated using a wax-resist method (batik). The designs are made with a stylus and beeswax.

Rozhovyny (also, *rozhoviny, rozhovinnia*) – The first of the non-Lenten meals, the *rozhovyny* takes place next day after Great Lent, which is Easter. This meal is filled with many rituals; one being that the first food that is consumed should be the one that was blessed at church, for example, *krashanky. Rozhivliatysia* is the verb referring to the act of *rozhovyny.*

Rushnyk (*rushnyky*, plural) – This Ukrainian ritual cloth is embroidered or woven with special designs. It plays a significant role in numerous traditional folk and family occasions, such as weddings, christenings and so on.

Salo – These are cured slabs of fatback (or pork belly).

Shynka – This is a synonym of *buzhenyna* (see definition).

Syr – (1) Literally translated as 'cheese', it may refer to any kind of cheese; (2) *Syr* also refers to a specific type of cheese that is very popular in Ukrainian cuisine, which is a type of quark made from soured cow milk.

Bibliography

Artiukh, L 1977, *Ukrainska Narodna Kulinaria* [Ukrainian Folk Cuisine], Naukova Dumka, Kyiv

Efymenko, P 1886, *Dnevnik Narodnykh Prazdnikov Kharkovskoy Hubernii: Kharkov Kalendar na 1887* [Diary of Folk Holidays of Kharkiv Province: Kharkiv Calendar for 1887], Kharkiv Provincial Government Publishing, Kharkiv

Klynovetska, Z 1991, *Stravy i Napytky na Ukraini* [Food and Beverages in Ukraine], Chas, Kyiv–Lviv, (reprint edition, first published in 1913)

Kylymnyk, S 1962, *Ukrainskyi Rik u Narodnykh Zvychayakh v Narodnomu Osvitlenni* [Ukrainian Year in Folk Customs from a Historical Perspective], Vol. 3, Winnipeg, Toronto

Markevych, M 1860, *Obychai, Poverya, Kukhnia i Napitki Malorossiyan* [Ukrainians' Customs, Folk Beliefs, Foods and Beverages] Davydenko Print, Kyiv

Shchelokovska, V 1899, 'Pishcha i Pitiyo Krestyan-Malorossov, s Nekotorymi Otnosiashchimisia Siuda Obychaiami, Poveryami i Primetami' [Ukrainian Villagers' Food and Beverages with Some Relevant Customs, Beliefs and Forewarnings], *Etnohraficheskoe Obozrenie* [Ethnographic Review], pp. 266–322

Shukhevych, V 1999, *Hutsulshchyna* [Hutsul Land], Vol. 4, Verkhovyna, Ivano-Frankivsk, (reprint edition, first published in 1904)

Skrypnyk, H, Bondarenko, H & Kurinna, M (eds.) 2016, *Etnohrafichnyi Obraz Suchasnoi Ukrainy. Korpus Ekspedytsijnykh Folklorno-Etnohrafichnykh Materialiv: Kalendarna Obriadovist* [Ethnographic Depiction of Modern Ukraine. Division of Folklore and Ethnography Expedition Materials: Ritual Calendar], The Rylsky Institute of Art Studies, Folklore and Ethnology, Kyiv

Sumtsov, M 1899, 'Kulturnye Perezhivaniya' [Cultural Experiences], *Kievskaya Starina* [Kyivan Antiquity], vol. 7, pp. 27–46

Voropaj, O 1958, *Zvychai Nashoho Narodu* [Customs of our People], Ukrainske Vydavnytstvo, Munich

Vovk, F 1928, *Studii z Ukrainskoi Etnohrafii ta Antropolohii* [Studies on Ukrainian Ethnography and Anthropology], Ukrainskyi Hromadskyi Vydavnychyi Fond, Prague

Tradition on a Plate Series

Yakovenko, Svitlana 2016, *Ukrainian Christmas Eve Supper: Traditional Village Recipes for Sviata Vecheria*, available in eBook format

Yakovenko, Svitlana 2017, *Ukrainian Ancient Grains: Recipes and Traditions,* coming soon in eBook format

More Titles from Sova Books

Yefymenko, Petro 2020, *A Collection of Ukrainian Spells*, available in hard copy format

Sumtsov, Mykola & ors 2019, *The Story of Pysanka: A Collection of Articles on Ukrainian Easter Eggs*, available in hard copy format

Sacher-Masoch, Leopold von and Haivoronskyi, Petro 2016, *Bloody Wedding in Kyiv: Two Tales of Olha, Kniahynia of Kyivan Rus*, available in eBook format

Somov, Orest 2016, *The Witches of Kyiv and Other Gothic Tales*, available in eBook format

Starytska-Cherniakhivska, Liudmyla 2015, *The Living Grave*, available in eBook format

Printed in Great Britain
by Amazon

84757518R00066